P9-AGM-654

BOLTS OF MELODY

NEW POEMS OF

EMILY DICKINSON

By Millicent Todd Bingham

ANCESTORS' BROCADES:

THE LITERARY DEBUT OF EMILY DICKINSON

Harper & Brothers, 1945

Edited by Mabel Loomis Todd

LETTERS OF EMILY DICKINSON:

NEW AND ENLARGED EDITION

Harper & Brothers, 1931

•

BOLTS OF MELODY

NEW POEMS OF

EMILY DICKINSON

EDITED BY

MABEL LOOMIS TODD

AND

MILLICENT TODD BINGHAM

NEW YORK, EVANSTON, AND LONDON
HARPER & ROW, PUBLISHERS

BOLTS OF MELODY

C-R

FOREWORD

No reader or student of Emily Dickinson needs to be told that the appearance of this book is an event of large importance. Several hundred hitherto unpublished works by one of the great poets of the world—almost any claim for such an event would amount to understatement. But in the present case there is the special interest, both literary and general, which attaches to any news of Emily Dickinson. For Mrs. Bingham's book is news of that mysterious person and that great poet, and it is news on so impressive a scale that one may well hesitate to improvise a statement of its value. The value of a fine poem—and many here are among Emily Dickinson's finest, even after years during which it might have been supposed that all the best were out—is scarcely to be stated anyhow. Such a poem states itself, as these immediately will to scholars, to poets, and to laymen in America who understand that Emily Dickinson is great not merely in their country but everywhere.

The task of editing her, as scholars at least are sure to know, is both a tease and a torment. The materials, the manuscripts, are either chaotic or elusive; sometimes they require so many decisions by the editor as to constitute him, provided his choices are wise, a poet himself; sometimes they seem to be clearer than they are, so that days of reflection will be necessary before a comma stays in or goes out. The breaking of lines, the dividing of stanzas, the working out of alternative phrases or words—these are but a few of the jobs to be done. Mrs. Bingham in her introduction has described them all with an accuracy which I am able to attest. It has been my privilege to watch Mrs. Bingham at work upon these poems, and it is my pleasure to say how much I admire the quality no less than the quantity of her devotion. Her mother, Mrs. Todd, was Emily Dickinson's first editor. She was superb in the rôle and Mrs. Bingham has everywhere been faithful to the challenge she inherited. The reader may have confidence that no problem has been skimped. Errors are always possible; Mrs. Bingham, I imagine, would be the last person to suggest that none had been made in this volume. But I can be witness to her sincere desire that the materials for their correction should be at the disposal of any student with a luckier eye or ear.

It is of course to be regretted that almost sixty years should have passed before poems of such distinction and beauty became available to the world. Emily Dickinson died in 1886. But all of that is a story in itself. Meanwhile, and finally, here the poems are.

MARK VAN DOREN

Falls Village, Connecticut
20 *October* 1944

INTRODUCTION

Your thoughts don't have words every day,
They come a single time
Like signal esoteric sips
Of sacramental wine,

Which while you taste so native seems,
So bounteous, so free,
You cannot comprehend its worth,
Nor its infrequency.

THE poems of Emily Dickinson were not published during her lifetime. It was only after her death in 1886 that the manuscripts were found by her sister Lavinia at whose request my mother, Mabel Loomis Todd, undertook the task of publication. With Thomas Wentworth Higginson she brought out the first volume, containing 116 poems, in 1890, and *Poems,* Second Series, in 1891. Without his help she published two volumes of letters, containing more than a hundred additional poems, in 1894, and *Poems,* Third Series, in 1896. Then, abruptly, her work stopped. Why? The answer to that question involves a long story. It is necessary to say here only that my mother had been alienated because of an irrelevant episode, a lawsuit about a strip of land brought against her by Lavinia Dickinson. As a consequence, nearly half of Emily's poems have remained unpublished to this day. The manuscripts which my mother was in process of preparing for the printer, together with all other documents relating to the Dickinson family, were put away—out of sight. For her it was the end of a chapter, one which she hoped to forget.

All these papers were packed in a camphor-wood chest. The lock, as you turn the key, plays a little tune. After the trial my mother locked the chest. It was not opened again until 1929 when, at her request, and with thumping heart, I turned the key and for the first time heard that little tune. What I might find within I did not know.

I looked and caught my breath. For there, before my eyes, were quantities of Emily's poems. How could they have kept quiet so long? With such inherent vitality it seemed as if they must have shouted, lying there in the dark all those years!

I closed the lid, locked the chest, and tried to take in the significance of what I had seen.

Students of Emily's poetry, disturbed by legends springing up about her, legends without basis of fact, had for several years been urging my mother to do something about it. But she refused. She was reluctant to return to the past. It was only after growing insistence from scholars that, mastering the ache of a lifetime, she finally consented to take up again the trail of long ago.

In order to straighten out the record the first step was to bring out a new edition of the 1894 *Letters of Emily Dickinson* since those volumes furnished the basis for an understanding of her life. Out of print for more than a generation, they must be made once more available. The new edition was published in 1931 and again took its place as the standard source book on the subject.[1]

We next planned a volume of previously unpublished poems. But the way should be prepared for so important a volume. The second step, therefore, must be a fully documented account of why publication ceased in 1896 and was not resumed by my mother. As a beginning, she and I read together her letters from Colonel Higginson and from the publishers, as well as all other correspondence about the original editing. That second step was halted midway. My mother died suddenly on October 14, 1932.

Of the reasons for the interruption of my mother's work in 1896 I had at the time of her death only the haziest idea. She did not talk about Dickinson relationships and animosities. It has required years to accumulate bits of information from widely scattered sources, to fit the story together piece by piece, and to

[1] *Letters of Emily Dickinson*, New and Enlarged Edition, edited by Mabel Loomis Todd, Harper & Brothers, 1931.

verify every fact before accepting it as part of the narrative. But the second step has at last been taken. The story of "Emily Dickinson's literary début," as my mother called it, has now been told.[2]

The present volume is the third step.

To return to the year 1929 and the camphor-wood chest. When I examined the contents—diaries, letters, and other Dickinson documents—I found also hundreds of poems. Some of them had been published, but many more were unpublished, including all those in this book.

The manuscripts of the poems were of two sorts: those Emily herself had worked over, and those which she had not touched since they were first captured in words—the "esoteric sips of sacramental wine." She had early begun to copy her poems and to destroy the rough drafts. She wrote them in ink on sheets of letter paper measuring five by eight inches. When she had filled five or six double sheets, she would make two pin-holes in the left margin and insert a piece of string, tying the sheets together in neat little fascicles which Lavinia called "volumes." This is the only way Emily tied up her poems. She never rolled them. Written at first in a fine running hand, the penmanship tends more and more to resemble the bold detached letters of the pencil script characteristic of her latest years. These fascicles contain the revised poems, including many which she apparently considered finished. During the last three years of my mother's life we went through them, while she told me incidents connected with her work forty years before. She had copied and edited the contents of all the fascicles and numbered them in blue pencil.

Although Emily seems to have considered many of these poems finished, as I have said, they were far from ready for the printer. The arrangement, verse form, and in particular the punctuation were not clearly indicated. In some poems dashes are sprinkled about so lavishly that they give to the page the appearance of a thread on which the phrases are strung. At times the dashes seem so integral a part of the text that an editor is tempted to perpetuate them, lest without them the words should fall apart.

[2] *Ancestors' Brocades, The Literary Début of Emily Dickinson,* Millicent Todd Bingham, Harper & Brothers, 1945.

In a good many poems she supplied alternative words, phrases, or lines, little crosses indicating where the final choice should be inserted. The editor is thus obliged to retrace Emily's steps, to follow the method she herself used, trying one word after another before deciding which best fits the particular setting. She admits that she sometimes approached the choice reluctantly.

> I hesitate which word to take, as I can take but few, and each must be the chiefest; but recall that Earth's most graphic transaction is placed within a syllable, nay, even a gaze.

An editor cannot indulge in the "luxury of doubt." He is forced to choose. All this my mother explained in an article written at the time of Emily's centenary.[3]

The success of the first volume of poems, published in November, 1890, had been so great that it spurred my mother to increased activity. By midsummer, 1891, all the poems that Emily had neatly written on sheets of letter paper had been copied and classified "A," "B," and "C." As soon as the manuscript of *Poems*, Second Series, was in the hands of the printer and before proof had begun to arrive, my mother made a list of all the poems she had copied except those in the two little volumes already published. The first lines were entered alphabetically in a small leather-covered notebook. In addition to those in the two volumes more than one thousand poems (including sixty-eight not listed in the notebook), were soon in shape for the printer. Of these, hundreds have not been published until now.

The 1891 list contains 926 first lines. But this number is only approximate because of duplication, as when one stanza from a longer poem is listed independently. For this, Emily herself is partly responsible. Many poems are easily broken into parts which can stand alone. She took advantage of this fact by sending to a friend a fragment to fit an occasion. Furthermore, she sometimes used the same stanza in two different poems. "When what they sung for is undone," the second stanza of "A pang is more conspicuous in spring," is also the beginning of another poem

[3] "Emily Dickinson's Literary Début," Mabel Loomis Todd, *Harper's Magazine*, March, 1930.

which trails off into a vague limbo. Such overlapping provides plenty of pitfalls for an unwary editor.

It should be noted that except for the elimination of alternatives my mother's copies follow Emily's manuscripts exactly, as shown by poems of which I have both the original and the copy. My mother was scrupulous about this. Any changes from the original text, whether of spelling or wording, were made subsequently on her own manuscripts and are plainly indicated. This makes her copies important, not only because they have correctly preserved a good many poems which might otherwise have been lost, but for another reason. Since they include the contents of *Further Poems* and *Unpublished Poems,* volumes brought out by Emily's niece, Martha Dickinson Bianchi, the copies serve until the originals again become available to check the accuracy of the published versions.

After my mother's death I re-examined the fascicles, comparing each poem with her copy of it. In making fresh copies of my own I did not always follow her editing, for I ignored her changes and sometimes disagreed with her choice of alternatives. My effort has always been to discover Emily's own preference. She had sometimes underlined one of the alternatives. But if no preference was indicated, in most cases I used the word she wrote first. In no single instance have I substituted a word or a phrase not suggested by Emily herself. Her spelling, on the other hand, has been standardized. Certain spellings had special meanings for Emily. But the something special evaporates in print. So, with great reluctance, I have changed archaic spelling to conform to current usage, substituting "dropped," for "dropt," for instance, and "gulf" for "gulph." But I have kept the word "phebe," itself a concession, for Emily said she saw it as "fee-bee."

As I look back upon it, transcription of poems in the fascicles seems like child's play in comparison with what was to follow. For nearly half of the poems in the present volume had not been edited nor, for the most part, even read by my mother. Let me explain.

In addition to the fascicles and some numbered loose sheets of letter paper not yet tied together, I found in the camphorwood chest many brown envelopes labeled "E.D., soon to be copied," "Very good odd scraps," "Copies being made, as yet unclassified," and so on. My mother did not tell me anything about the contents of these envelopes except that they contained odds and ends which but for a few she had not looked at. She always referred to them as "scraps," not to disparage the poems, but to describe the bits of paper on which they were written. We did not attempt to decipher them, but laid them aside as she had done a generation earlier, and as I for several years continued to do. Their appearance was so discouraging that I put off grappling with them from year to year, wondering indeed as I did so whether I should ever attempt to disentangle them, whether the time required would not be wasted. It is only during the last three years that I have finally made a systematic examination of the contents of those envelopes.

The result has been the discovery of some of Emily's finest poetry, because these are the poems she wrote in her fullest maturity. They are all in the latest handwriting and all in pencil. None of the poems of the final phase of her life were copied by her in ink and tied in fascicles. Many of them, though obviously first drafts, are nevertheless perfect poems without suggested change of a word or a syllable, needing only to be deciphered. It is precisely because, during her last years, these thoughts were jotted down at white heat and never revised that some of her most powerful poems, dealing with fundamental areas of experience, are contained in this volume. Like the dormant life-germ of a plant these verses, buried for sixty years, are at last reaching light and air in full vitality.

But when first discovered they looked impossible—a jumble of words on odds and ends of paper, some of it crumpled and torn. They were not sorted alphabetically, or according to size, or subject matter, or date of composition. Most of them were smothered with alternative words and phrases crowded into every available space—around the edges, upside down, wedged between the lines. Some poems, filling the margins of drafts of letters to friends, are difficult to distinguish from the body of the letter, following without a break on the same sheet of paper. Many are written on the backs of brown-paper bags or of discarded bills, programs, and invitations; on tiny scraps of station-

Contained in this short
~~Combined~~
Comprised Life

Are six wonderful notes.
are magical
fairies
miraculous

Visionings to not a friend
Vast Omnipotence
A friend to straight
to sleep
the distant subtle to be seen
Come unto me masked
accomplished
how
With the moments between
Centuries

The soul came home
to sleep
at night from his
towns
that would scenes
un to sense I
have dazzled
As doth the tired sense
un manifest to sense
Unwitnessed of the sense

Span
visitors were
Centuries

Facsimile of poem on page 265

Contained in this short life
are magical extents both
the soul returning soft as
night skies by become
to skies securer thence
or sunrise strictest
As children strictly kept
take lesson surest to go the sea
Whose waters are the howling nameless
brook
to thine infinity
Beside Infinity
Whose nameless fathoms
slink away
Beside infinity

Contained in
this short life
are magical
extents
the soul returning
soft at night
to skies securer
thence
as children kept
strictest soonest to
turn the sea
Whose nameless
fathoms slink
away
Beside infinity

ery pinned together; on leaves torn from old notebooks (one such sheet dated "1824"); on soiled and mildewed subscription blanks, or on department- or drug-store bargain flyers from Amherst and surrounding towns. There are pink scraps, blue and yellow scraps, one of them a wrapper of *Chocolat Meunier*; poems on the reverse of recipes in her own writing, on household shopping lists, on the cut-off margins of newspapers, and on the inside of their brown-paper wrappings. The poem,

> Oh, give it motion! Deck it sweet
> With artery and vein!

complete, without suggested change, is on the reverse of a printed slip which reads:

> This Lamp, bearing upon the Chimney Gallery and upon the Thumbscrew, the name of *The German Student Lamp Co.*, is hereby guaranteed to be perfect in all its parts, to burn properly and not to leak.
>
> Should this Lamp not fulfill this Guarantee, another will be supplied in its place.

Emily liked best the inside of used envelopes. Some were addressed to herself or Lavinia, or to their parents, the canceled stamps still attached; others, addressed to friends, had never been posted. Many a detached flap, too, provided just room enough for one perfect quatrain. Often the writing is clear and distinct. On other scraps it is so confused that it looks as if written in the dark—lines overlapping, letters half formed. Indeed, it is sometimes impossible to tell whether such lines constitute a single poem, or whether two or more were intended as with "Contained in this short life," here reproduced in facsimile, which might be two poems, or two versions of the same poem, or a single poem of two stanzas, as on page 265. The sequence of lines, too, is often difficult to determine; in some cases even the first line may be in doubt. But after laboriously puzzling out a word, a line, a stanza, letter by letter, with all the alternatives, one is rewarded by seeing, suddenly, a perfect poem burst full-blown into life. The clarity of the thought shines forth in striking contrast to the chaos of the manuscript.

Three poems, reproduced in facsimile herewith, make further

A Sparrow took a
slice of Twig
And ~~thought~~ it very nice
I think, because his
empty Plate
Was handed Nature twice.

Invigorated fully - sprang
lightly to the sky
As an accustomed
stirrup - and rode Immensity
And boldly rode away -

And rode deriding by -

fluently
Absconded daintily.
the Epicure of Courtes,
Purposes
As of Amenity.
Propriety

the Epicure of Firmaments
As of Frugality.

Facsimile of poem I on page xxii

Rose softly in the sky
As a familiar Stirrup
to mount Immensity -

And gaily galloped by -

the Epicure of Vehicles
As of Velocity.

— — — — —

As Speculations flee
By no Conclusion
hindered Derision
~~Left~~ - - Rose surreptitiously -

turned easy in the sky
As a familiar saddle -

And rode Immensity -

x to Every Heaven above
+ to all the Saints he knew
every God he knew

The Bobolink
is gone - the
Rowdy of the
Meadow -
And no one
swaggers now
but me -
The Presbyterian
Birds can now
resume the Meeting
He gaily [boldly] interrup-
ted + ~~that~~ overflowing
Day
When opening the
Sabbath in their
afflictive Way
He bowed to
Heaven instead
of Earth -
And shouted
Let us pray -
and shouted let us pray -

He recognized his maker - overturned the Decalogue -

Facsimile of poem II on page xxii

He sung upon
the Decalogue
And shouted
Let us pray—
When supplicating mercy
In a portentous
way.

portentous
in a

Sat from an unanni-
ointed Twig
He gargled—bubbled
Let us pray—
Smut—ahem a
surreptitious Twig

Two Butterflies went
out at Noon
And waltzed upon
a Farm.
And then espied
Circumference
And caught a ride
with him.
Then lost themselves
And found themselves
In eddies of the Sun
Fathoms in
Till Rapture missed them
Peninsula. Gravitation
chased
And Both were wrecked
in Noon.
To all surviving Butterflies
Be this Fatuity
Example. and monition
to entomology.

Till Gravitation humbled — Ejected them

soon — away

Facsimile of poem III on page xxii

+ then overlook — and
took a Boat with him.
+ In Rapids of the Sun
+ missed her footing —
+ Drowned — quenched —
whelmed — in noon —
+ this Biography —

Until a Zephyr — flung —
pushed them — spurned
chased — — then staked
[illegible] themselves and
Until a — lost ~~Themselves~~
Zephyr scourged — in Gambols
them — with of the
And they + — Sun — travesties
were hurled S — ties
from noon — for travesty
then chased — of the Sun
themselves and — gambols
caught — antics
themselves — in with the Sun

[illegible]

elaboration of editorial difficulties superfluous. Out of these manuscripts the following poems have emerged.

I

A sparrow took a slice of twig
And thought it very nice,
I think, because his empty plate
Was handed nature twice.

Invigorated fully,
Turned easy in the sky
As a familiar saddle,
And rode immensity.

II

The bobolink is gone,
The rowdy of the meadow,
And no one swaggers now but me;
The Presbyterian birds
Can now resume the meeting
He gaily interrupted
That overflowing day
When, opening the Sabbath
In their afflictive way,
He swung upon the decalogue
And shouted, "Let us pray!"

III

Two butterflies went out at noon
And waltzed upon a farm,
And then espied circumference
And caught a ride with him;

Then lost themselves and found themselves
In eddies of the sun,
Till rapture missed her footing
And both were wrecked in noon.

To all surviving butterflies
Be this biography,
Example, and monition
To entomology.

In a simplified transcription of the manuscript of Poem III, with every alternative word placed where it belongs except "peninsula," the phrases in italics are those selected by the editor.[4]

[4] Stanza 1 Two butterflies went out at noon

And waltzed upon a farm,

And then espied circumference
Then overtook circumference

And caught a ride with him;
And took a bout with him

Stanza 2 *Then lost themselves and found themselves*
Then staked themselves and lost themselves
Then chased themselves and caught themselves

In eddies of the sun,
In fathoms in the sun
In rapids of the sun
In gambols with (of) the sun
In frenzies with (of) the sun
For frenzy of the sun
In antics (gambols) in (with) the sun

Till rapture missed her footing
Till gravitation missed (chased) them
Till gravitation humbled (ejected) them
Till gravitation foundered (grumbled)
Until a zephyr pushed (chased) (flung) (spurned) them
Until a zephyr scourged them

And both were wrecked in noon.
And both were drowned (quenched) (whelmed) in noon
And they were hurled from noon

Stanza 3 To all surviving butterflies

Be this fatuity
Be this biography,

Example, and monition

To entomology.

A different version of this poem was published in *Poems,* Second Series, p. 133.

The poems of Emily Dickinson should eventually be arranged in the order of composition as well as by subject matter as heretofore. Her inner development would thus become apparent—the gradual turning from acute personal feeling to emotion universal in scope. Toward the last only that concerned her. Most rewarding would be a comparison of poems about death—the long discursive poems of youth such as "The feet of people walking home" and "There is a morn by men unseen"—with the terse direct quatrains of the final years, those comprehensive generalizations narrowed to four short lines:

The vastest earthly day
Is shrunken small
By one defaulting face
Behind a pall.

Some of Emily's latest poems on fame, a rather cool topic, to be sure, but one which contrary to common belief nagged her incessantly, further illustrate what chronological arrangement can reveal.

Because Emily Dickinson refused to publish, it has been assumed that she did not care for fame. By way of evidence to the contrary, poems found among these latest scraps prove that she was obsessed by the thought of it. Indeed, she was so conscious that she deserved it that she had to keep continually reminding herself of its futility—that her own approval was all that mattered.

Fame of myself to justify!
All other plaudit be
Superfluous, an incense
Beyond necessity.

Fame of myself to lack, although
My name be else supreme,
This were an honor honorless,
A futile diadem.

She was aware that among one's contemporaries fame comes slowly if at all, and she shielded her poems from their indifference. "Too near thou art for fame" is her way of putting it.

In addition to her published poems on this subject I have

before me fifteen new poems dealing with fame. The earliest of these, in the handwriting of the seventies, show a somewhat cynical attitude toward the transient quality of what she calls "the incident of fame."

> Fame is the tint that scholars leave
> Upon their setting names,
> The iris not of occident
> That disappears as comes.

The frog is a symbol of its evanescence—already a familiar thought in "I'm nobody—who are you?" She mentions "his eloquence a bubble, as fame should be," but in another poem amplifies its true nature:

> A clover's simple fame
> Remembered of the cow
> Is sweeter than enameled realms
> Of notoriety.
>
> Renown perceives itself
> And that profanes the flower;
> The daisy that has looked behind
> Has compromised its power.

She contrasts the desire for fame with achievement worthy of it:

> The beggar at the door for fame
> Were easily supplied,
> But bread is that diviner thing,
> Disclosed to be denied.

Like happiness, fame cannot be achieved by seeking it:

> To earn it by disdaining it
> Is fame's consummate fee.

All this Emily knew very well. And yet the thought of fame possessed her. It would not let her go. She questioned whether death is indeed its prerequisite.

> The first we knew of him was death,
> The second was renown;
> Except the first had justified,
> The second had not been.

Is the quality of a man's work really discernible only after he is gone?

All men for honor hardest work,
But are not known to earn,
Paid after they have ceased to work
In infamy or urn.

That thought is expressed over and over again:

Above oblivion's tide there is a pier,
And an effaceless few are lifted there,
Nay, lift themselves; fame has no arms,
And but one smile inlaid with balms.

Once more:

Fame is the one that does not stay;
Its occupant must die,
Or out of sight of estimate
Ascend incessantly,

Or be that most insolvent thing,
A lightning in the germ—
Electrical the embryo
Or findless is the flame.

Assuming that her poems must ultimately find an audience, Emily declared her faith in the appraisal of posterity in one last mighty affirmation:

The poets light but lamps,
Themselves go out;
The wicks they stimulate,
If vital light

Inhere, as do the suns,
Each age a lens
Disseminating their
Circumference.

Not all the poems belong in the body of the book. Part Two contains those which are incomplete, fragmentary, or trivial. It is as true of them as of all her poems that though Emily attached importance to form, she had her own rules. Some of her finished poems are rough, rugged, awkward. But that she intended. In some of these unfinished poems, however, not only is the idea obscured by the form; the idea itself is obscure—not sharp enough to pierce through the words. It may be questioned whether such gropings should be published at all. Many of them will undoubtedly not appear in a final edition. But the fact remains that through some of the most confused passages shines a thought so searching that it should be preserved whatever the setting.

To select the poems for a definitive edition of the works of Emily Dickinson will be easier in fifty years than it is now. At present, even the best of critics differ as to which ones should be included. In so far as publication is concerned, the day for an editorial sieve has passed. The poems should be given an equal chance at survival. And so, all unpublished poems and fragments of which I have copies are included in this book. All, that is, except for a group of about fifty poems hitherto published only in part. These must wait for restoration of the omitted portions —sometimes amounting to as much as four stanzas—until all of Emily's manuscripts are accessible, so that each poem can once more be compared with the original and a truly definitive edition compiled.[5]

[5] Volumes containing poems by Emily Dickinson:

Poems by Emily Dickinson, edited by Mabel Loomis Todd and T. W. Higginson, 1890

Poems, Second Series, edited by T. W. Higginson and Mabel Loomis Todd, 1891

Letters of Emily Dickinson, edited by Mabel Loomis Todd, 1894, 2 vols.

Poems, Third Series, edited by Mabel Loomis Todd, 1896

The Single Hound, edited by Martha Dickinson Bianchi, 1914

The Life and Letters of Emily Dickinson, by Martha Dickinson Bianchi, 1924

Further Poems of Emily Dickinson, edited by Martha Dickinson Bianchi and Alfred Leete Hampson, 1929

Letters of Emily Dickinson, New and Enlarged Edition, edited by Mabel Loomis Todd, 1931

Emily Dickinson, Face to Face, by Martha Dickinson Bianchi, 1932

Unpublished Poems of Emily Dickinson, edited by Martha Dickinson Bianchi and Alfred Leete Hampson, 1935

The Poems of Emily Dickinson (current collected edition), edited by Martha Dickinson Bianchi and Alfred Leete Hampson, 1937

Ancestors' Brocades, The Literary Début of Emily Dickinson, by Millicent Todd Bingham, 1945

On the whole, the impression gained from working with Emily's poems through the years is of a lavishness, a fecundity, comparable to the prodigality of nature, scattering a thousand seeds to insure the survival of one. It is not hard to imagine Lavinia Dickinson's consternation when, after her sister's death, she first discovered the manuscripts.

Emily died leaving no instructions as to what should be done with her poems. She did not ask to have them published, nor—a fact which should be emphasized—did she ask to have them destroyed. Her part in them finished, she recklessly confided her life's work to the cosmos. Was it recklessness, I wonder, or was it faith? If the latter, her confidence in their survival would seem to have been hardly justified. Lavinia would find them of course. But what could she do with them? Her sole qualification for custody of so stupendous a treasure was that she worshiped Emily with a fierce and jealous loyalty. The poems must be published. That Lavinia knew. But how? She made up in resoluteness what she lacked in knowledge.

It is by a lucky chance that in Amherst, at that time a remote village, a person should have been at hand who had the necessary sensitivity, skill, patience, and capacity for long-sustained hard work, as well as the willingness to devote years to the task of editing. It is luckier still that the same person should have been able to appreciate the grandeur of the poetry, to believe in it to such a degree that in spite of its flouting the standards of Victorian verse, and against the advice of publisher and critic, she nevertheless went ahead, preparing manuscripts for the printer, sustained by her own conviction that she was dealing with "the greater glory." It is interesting to speculate as to what might have happened to the poems of Emily Dickinson had Mrs. Todd not been at hand.

Given to my mother by Lavinia Dickinson to publish, halted on their way to the press by an imbroglio unrelated to literature, the poems in this volume are at last released to a public which should no longer be denied the right to enjoy them.

M.T.B.

Washington, D.C.
20 *October* 1944

CONTENTS

PART ONE

I would not paint a picture.
I'd rather be the one
Its bright impossibility
To dwell delicious on,
And wonder how the fingers feel
Whose rare celestial stir
Evokes so sweet a torment,
Such sumptuous despair.

I would not talk like cornets.
I'd rather be the one
Raised softly to horizons
And out, and easy on
Through villages of ether,
Myself endued balloon
By but a lip of metal,
The pier to my pontoon.

Nor would I be a poet.
It's finer own the ear,
Enamored, impotent, content
The license to revere—
A privilege so awful
What would the dower be
Had I the art to stun myself
With bolts of melody!

PART ONE

NOTHING reveals the scope of Emily Dickinson's insight more than the variety of her themes. This I have attempted to bring out by the arrangement of the poems in this book.

The poems in Part One have been grouped in such a way that the subject matter progresses toward a climax. First comes the world without, nature in its various aspects; the circuit of a day, of a year; weather; animals and plants. So great is the renewal of spirit gained from nature that Emily could exclaim in some surprise,

> I thought that nature was enough
> Till human nature came!

So next are the Ages of Man: childhood; the awakening of emotion, of romantic love; some poignant stanzas about other human beings, and finally meditations on the mystery of death. All the foregoing lead up to three groups of philosophical poems which open vistas into the significance of life. These culminate in "An Ablative Estate," a section in which more than half of the poems, among them the greatest, were written during the last years of Emily's life.

The poems are arranged under twelve main headings.

The Far Theatricals of Day

Dawn, sunrise, noon; the bland quiet of a summer afternoon; the marshaling of cloud, the rising wind, the beat of rain; lightning, thunder, the "conflict of the upper friends," subsiding at last as "the day fades from the firmament away" into slow-moving night—moon, stars, will-o'-the-wisps and all "the apparatus of the dark."

The Round Year

"The transient, fragrant snow" of late winter is followed by spring, "the period express from God"; "the pomp of summer days"; "September's baccalaureate," harvest time and Indian summer; the "early, stooping night" of November and winter with "his hoar delights."

My Pageantry

Garden "pageantry" sown in May, "bestowed a summer long," is finally overtaken by "the frost, himself so comely," which "dishevels every prime."

Our Little Kinsmen

Emily contemplates "several of nature's people," frogs, birds, spiders, squirrels, rats, angleworms, and insects—"the most important population"—"with modesties enlarged."

Once a Child

Except for a few written in the first person, most of these poems in and about childhood deal with small boys.

The Mob within the Heart

Many of these poems were written comparatively early in life when personal desire loomed large and other people had the power to "mangle." Dealing with personal emotion as it does, the section is frankly autobiographical, beginning with the quality of childhood loneliness, devotion to girlhood friends, disappointment in a too-much-loved woman friend, "bandaged moments" and the effort to forget, followed by two or three poems on the anatomy of disenchantment. After the passage of time comes emancipation from the feeling of loneliness, and with it a sense of escape and the exhilaration of discovery that

> The staple must be optional
> That an immortal binds.

In this release from dependence on "mortal company" Emily found the friends who do not fail, and in so doing achieved that confidence and mellow humor which is in reality a sense of proportion. Her detachment was not completely successful, however, for the final poem, a cry of exasperation, is in the very latest handwriting.

Italic Faces

These poems describe specific persons, some of them historical.

The Infinite Aurora

First among these love poems are those written in youth—the awakening of romantic love, exultation in it, the torture of separation—all with a very special person in mind. After a while, Emily is able to dissect the vital experience, to define what it is, how it happens. Youthful rhapsodies gradually give way to a sense of "the royal infinity,"

> Love is the fellow of the resurrection
> Scooping up the dust and chanting "Live!"

The White Exploit

In this section the Ages of Man come full circle. From the time when Emily Dickinson first began to write poetry until her last fading pencil marks on tattered bits of paper, the mystery of death absorbed her. Her poems about death are divided into six parts:

> THE FINAL INCH: These poems deal with the physical fact —ways in which a man may die. In early handwriting, most of the poems are concerned with a specific individual and "the manner of its death."
>
> THE SILVER RETICENCE: Here is the expression of personal feeling aroused by the spectacle of death. Some of these poems appear to have been written in its very presence—at her mother's bier. Even Emily's deepest emotions sought refuge in words.
>
> REPEALED FROM OBSERVATION: These are meditations on the great gulf that separates us from loved ones who have "ceased," and the yearning for an answer from "kindred

as responsive as porcelain." The final poem in this group might well stand as the valedictory of the present crisis in human history.

LIDS OF STEEL: This is the grave—"the finished feeling" experienced when the "lid" has closed upon a friend, but somewhat depersonalized in speculation concerning the stranger-dead.

CONCLUDED LIVES: A few poems in this section express grief for "the finished creatures departed me," but on the whole they seem strangely detached, written during the pause allotted after the death of a friend in which "our faith to regulate."

CREATURES CLAD IN MIRACLE: These are they who "go up by two and two" to meet the "torrents of eternity." Beginning with doubt as to the reality of heaven and the inhabitants thereof, the section culminates in a mighty certainty, confidence in a time "when questions are not needed for answers." To accentuate Emily's gradual change of attitude toward the hereafter I have placed near the end a youthful rhapsody, "There is a morn by men unseen," among poems of the latest period. Written in pencil on crumpled scraps of paper, these short, late poems bear an affirmation as serene and steady as the Psalms.

Vital Light

These poems have to do with the nature of inspiration and its elusiveness, the "bequest of wings." It is the "vital light"—in beauty, in truth, in poetry, in all creative art. Here is another of those great affirmations of Emily's last years compacted in four lines:

> Estranged from beauty none can be
> For beauty is infinity,
> And power to be finite ceased
> When fate incorporated us.

The section concludes with the assurance that when genius is true to itself, it eventuates in fame. It "cannot escape her."

That Campaign Inscrutable

Emotion in the abstract is depicted here, the complement of similar feelings narrowed to a person in the section entitled *The Mob within the Heart.* But though expressed in generalizations the feeling does not lose in intensity. Here are whole areas of experience: hope, joy, happiness, gratitude, loneliness, patience, and their interrelationships; the rôle of silence and of escape, grief, anguish, and the nature of failure and despair.

An Ablative Estate

"The web of life" is here surveyed by an onlooker, by one who stands "on the tops of things and like the trees" looks down, but who looks through "triple lenses." The "magical extents" of life are explored with a fine detachment, as though from beyond a battle fought through. The generalizations are objective and impersonal, dealing with such realms as the enticement of mystery and the dullness of certainty; the danger of over-indulgence in memory "shod with adamant"; also with the nature of various ingratiating traits, each summed up in a few words—wonder, faith, surprise, suspense, the joy of risk and experiment which "escorts us last." The everlasting anomalies of life are somewhat mitigated by the unescapable presence of the soul. In bygone years the faith of the Puritans held firm. The final poem in Part One summarizes in eight lines the ebbing strength which follows loss of faith such as theirs.

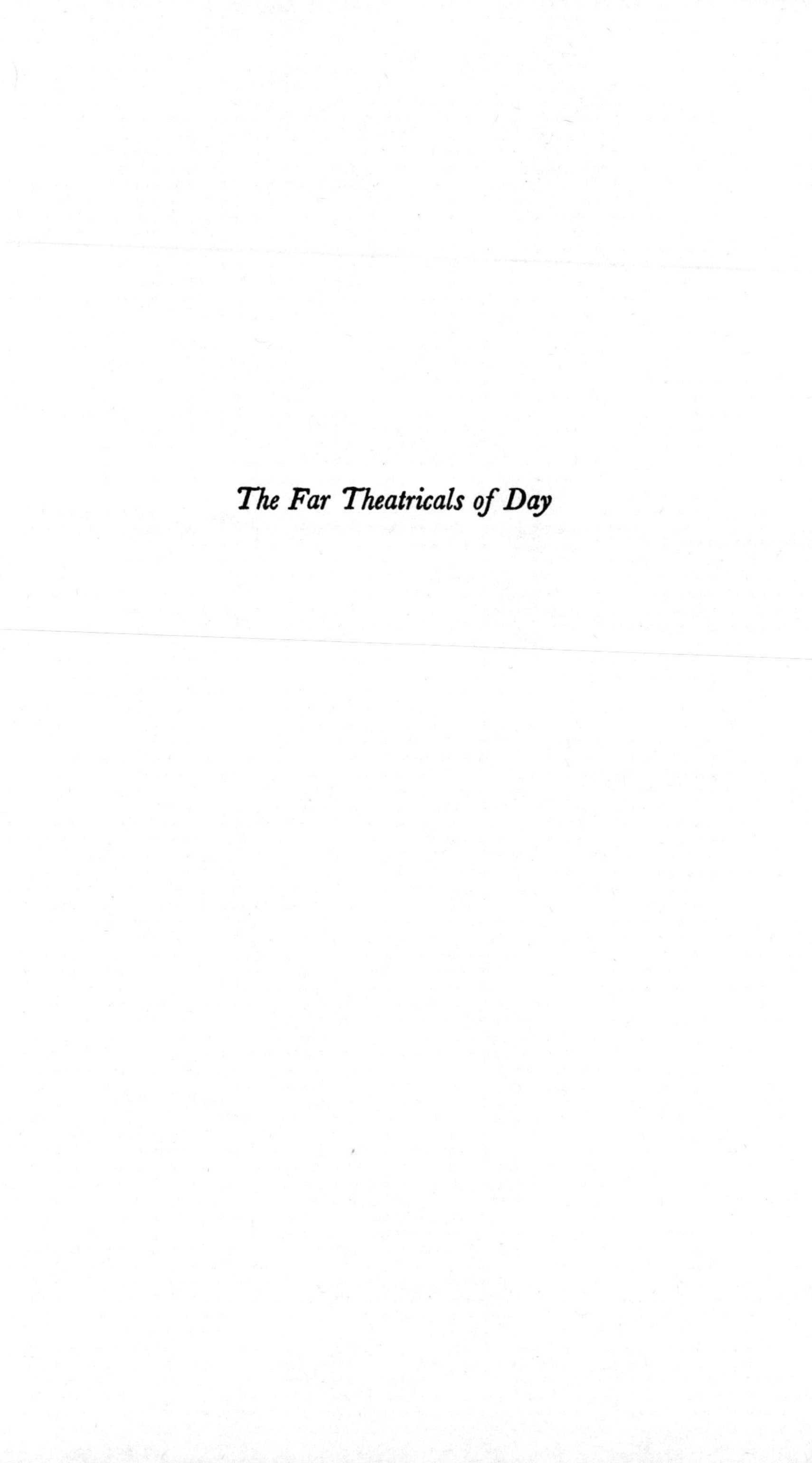

The Far Theatricals of Day

· 1 ·

THE fingers of the light
Tapped soft upon the town
With, "I am great and cannot wait,
So therefore let me in."

"You're soon," the town replied,
"My faces are asleep.
But swear, and I will let you by,
You will not wake them up."

The easy guest complied,
But once within the town,
The transport of his countenance
Awakened maid and man.

The neighbor in the pool,
Upon his hip elate,
Made loud obeisance, and the gnat
Held up his cup for light.

· 2 ·

THE birds begun at four o'clock—
Their period for dawn—
A music numerous as space
And measureless as noon.

I could not count their force,
Their voices did expend
As brook by brook bestows itself
To magnify the pond.

Their listener was none
Except occasional man
In homely industry arrayed
To overtake the morn.

Nor was it for applause
That I could ascertain,
But independent ecstasy
Of universe and men.

By six the flood had done,
No tumult there had been
Of dressing or departure,
Yet all the band was gone.

The sun engrossed the east,
The day controlled the world,
The miracle that introduced
Forgotten as fulfilled.

· 3 ·

THE pattern of the sun
Can fit but him alone,
For sheen must have a disk
To be a sun.

· 4 ·

A DAY! Help! Help! Another day!
Your prayers, oh, passer-by!
From such a common ball as this
Might date a victory!

From marshalings as simple
The flags of nations swang.
Steady, my soul—what issues
Upon thine arrow hang!

· 5 ·

WHEN I have seen the sun emerge
From his amazing house
And leave a day at every door,
A deed in every place,

Without the incident of fame
Or accident of noise,
The earth has seemed to me a drum
Pursued of little boys.

· 6 ·

How good his lava bed
To this laborious boy
Who must be up to call the world
And dress the sleepy day!

· 7 ·

WHO saw no sunrise cannot say
The countenance 'twould be;
Who guess at seeing, guess at loss
Of the ability.

The emigrant of light, it is
Afflicted for the day,
The blindness that beheld and blest
And could not find its eye.

· 8 ·

MORNING that comes but once
Considers coming twice.
Two dawns upon a single morn
Make life a sudden price.

· 9 ·

THE sun is one, and on the tare
He doth as punctual call
As on the conscientious flower,
And estimates them all.

· 10 ·

THE bird did prance, the bee did play,
The sun ran miles away,
So blind with joy he could not choose
Between his holiday;

The morn was up, the meadows out,
The fences all but ran—
Republic of delight, I thought,
Where each is citizen.

From heavy-laden lands to thee
Were seas to cross to come,
A Caspian were crowded—
Too near thou art for fame.

· 11 ·

THE sun and fog contested
The government of day.
The sun took down his yellow whip
And drove the fog away.

· 12 ·

LIGHT is sufficient to itself.
If others want to see,
It can be had on window panes
Some hours of the day,

But not for compensation—
It holds as large a glow
To squirrel in the Himmaleh
Precisely, as to you.

· 13 ·

NOON is the hinge of day,
Evening the folding door,
Morning, the east compelling the sill
Till all the world is ajar.

· 14 ·

RESTS at night the sun from shining,
Nature,
And some men;

Rest at noon some men, while nature
And the sun
Go on.

· 15 ·

A CLOUD withdrew from the sky.
Superior glory be,
But that cloud and its auxiliaries
Are forever lost to me.

Had I but further scanned,
Had I secured the glow
In an hermetic memory
It had availed me now.

Never to pass the angel
With a glance and a bow
Till I am firm in heaven
Is my intention now.

· 16 ·

A CURIOUS cloud surprised the sky,
'Twas like a sheet with horns;
The sheet was blue, the antlers gray,
It almost touched the lawns

So low it leaned, then statelier drew,
And trailed like robes away—
A queen adown a satin aisle
Had not the majesty.

· 17 ·

A SOUTH wind has a pathos
Of individual voice,
As one detect on landings
An emigrant's address,

A hint of ports and peoples,
And much not understood,
The fairer for the farness
And for the foreignhood.

· 18 ·

It was a quiet seeming day,
There was no harm in earth or sky
Till with the setting sun
There strayed an accidental red,
A strolling hue one would have said,
To westward of the town.

But when the earth began to jar
And houses vanished with a roar
And human nature hid,
We comprehended by the awe,
As those that dissolution saw,
The warrant in the cloud.

· 19 ·

A wild blue sky abreast of winds
That threatened it did run,
And crouched behind his yellow door
Sat the defiant sun—

Some conflict with those upper friends
So genial in the main
That we deplore peculiarly
This arrogant campaign.

· 20 ·

The lightning is a yellow fork
From tables in the sky
By inadvertent fingers dropped,
The awful cutlery

Of mansions never quite disclosed
And never quite concealed,
The apparatus of the dark
To ignorance revealed.

· 21 ·

THE lightning playeth all the while,
But when he singeth, then
Ourselves are conscious he exist,
And we approach him stern,

With insulators and a glove,
Whose short sepulchral bass
Alarms us, though his yellow feet
May pass and counterpass

Upon the ropes above our head
Continual, with the news,
Nor we so much as check our speech
Nor stop to cross ourselves.

· 22 ·

LIKE rain it sounded till it curved,
And then I knew 'twas wind;
It walked as wet as any wave
But swept as dry as sand.

When it had pushed itself away
To some remotest plain
A coming as of hosts was heard—
That was indeed the rain!

It filled the wells, it pleased the pools,
It warbled in the road,
It pulled the spigot from the hills
And let the floods abroad;

It loosened acres, lifted seas,
The sites of centers stirred,
Then like Elijah rode away
Upon a wheel of cloud.

· 23 ·

THE wind took up the northern things
And piled them in the south,
Then bent the east unto the west
And, opening his mouth,

The four divisions of the earth
Did make as to devour,
While everything to corners slunk
Behind the awful power.

The wind unto his chambers went,
And nature ventured out,
Her subjects scattered into place,
Her systems ranged about;

Again the smoke from dwellings rose
The day abroad was heard.
How intimate, a tempest past,
The transport of the bird!

· 24 ·

THEIR barricade against the sky
The martial trees withdraw,
And with a flag at every turn
Their armies are no more.

What russet halts in nature's march
They indicate or cause,
An inference of Mexico
Effaces the surmise.

Recurrent to the after mind
That massacre of air,
The wound that was not wound nor scar,
But holidays of war.

· 25 ·

THEY called me to the window, for
'Twas sunset, someone said.
I only saw an amber farm
And just a single herd

Of opal cattle feeding far
Upon so vain a hill
As even while I looked dissolved,
Nor cattle were, nor soil,

But in their stead a sea displayed,
And ships of such a size
As crew of mountains could afford
And decks to seat the skies.

This too the showman rubbed away,
And when I looked again,
Nor farm, nor opal herd was there,
Nor Mediterranean.

· 26 ·

THAT's the Battle of Burgoyne,
Over every day
By the time that man and beast
Put their work away.

"Sunset" sounds majestic,
But that solemn war
Could you comprehend it
You would chastened stare.

· 27 ·

"RED SEA," indeed! Talk not to me
Of purple Pharaoh,
I have a navy in the west
Would pierce his columns through,

Guileless, yet of such glory fine
That all along the line,
Is it, or is it not, marine?
Is it, or not, divine?

The eye inquires with a sigh
That earth should be so big.
What exultation in the woe,
What wine in the fatigue!

· 28 ·

WHO is the east? The yellow man
Who may be purple if he can,
That carries in the sun.

Who is the west? The purple man
Who may be yellow if he can,
That lets him out again.

· 29 ·

SUNSET that screens, reveals,
Enhancing what we see
By menaces of amethyst
And moats of mystery.

· 30 ·

THE lilac is an ancient shrub,
But ancienter than that
The firmamental lilac
Upon the hill tonight.

The sun subsiding on his course
Bequeathes this final plant
To contemplation—not to touch—
The flower of occident.

Of one corolla is the west,
The calyx is the earth,
The capsule's burnished seeds, the stars.
The scientist of faith

His research has but just begun;
Above his synthesis
The flora unimpeachable
To time's analysis.

"Eye hath not seen" may possibly
Be current with the blind,
But let not revelation
By theses be detained.

· 31 ·

The sun kept stooping, stooping, low,
The hills to meet him rose.
On his side what transaction!
On their side what repose!
Deeper and deeper grew the stain
Upon the window pane,
Thicker and thicker stood the feet
Until the Tyrian
Was crowded dense with armies,
So gay, so brigadier,
That I felt martial stirrings
Who once the cockade wore,
Charged from my chimney corner—
But nobody was there!

· 32 ·

The sunset stopped on cottages
Where sunset hence must be
For treason not of his, but life's,
Gone westerly today.

The sunset stopped on cottages
Where morning just begun.
What difference after all thou mak'st,
Thou supercilious sun!

· 33 ·

Whole gulfs of red and fleets of red
And crews of solid blood
Did place about the west tonight
As 'twere a signal ground,

And they, appointed creatures
In authorized arrays
Due, promptly as a drama
That bows and disappears.

· 34 ·

THE color of a queen is this—
The color of a sun
At setting, this and amber;
Beryl and this at noon;

And when at night auroran widths
Fling suddenly on men,
'Tis this and witchcraft—nature has
An awe of iodine.

· 35 ·

SWEET mountains, ye tell me no lie,
Never deny me, never fly.
Those same unvarying eyes
Turn on me, when I fail or feign
Or take the royal names in vain,
Their far, slow, violet gaze.

My strong madonnas cherish still
The wayward nun beneath the hill
Whose service is to you,
Her latest worship when the day
Fades from the firmament away
To lift her brows on you.

· 36 ·

THE mountains stood in haze,
The valleys stopped below,
And went or waited as they liked
The river and the sky.

At leisure was the sun,
His interests of fire
A little from remark withdrawn.
The twilight spoke the spire.

So soft upon the scene
The act of evening fell
We felt how neighborly a thing
Was the invisible.

· 37 ·

AS WILLING lid o'er weary eye,
The evening on the day
Leans till of all our nature's house
Remains but balcony.

· 38 ·

FAIRER through fading, as the day
Into the darkness dips away,
Half her complexion of the sun
Hindering, haunting, perishing,

Rallies her glow like a dying friend,
Teasing with glittering amend,
Only to aggravate the dark
Through an expiring perfect look.

· 39 ·

THIS slow day moved along,
I heard its axles go
As if they could not hoist themselves
They hated motion so.

I told my soul to come,
It was no use to wait,
We went and played and came again—
And it was out of sight.

· 40 ·

THE sun and moon must make their haste
The stars express around,
For in the zones of paradise
The Lord alone is burned.

His eye it is the East and West;
The North and South, when He
Do concentrate His countenance,
Like glowworms flee away.

Oh, poor and far, oh, hindered eye
That hunted for the day—
The Lord a candle entertains
Entirely for thee!

· 41 ·

IT RISES, passes, on our south
Inscribes a simple noon,
Cajoles a moment with the spires,
And, infinite, is gone.

· 42 ·

THE red blaze is the morning,
The violet is noon,
The yellow, day is falling,
And after that is none.

But miles of sparks at evening
Reveal the width that burned—
The territory argent
That never yet consumed.

· 43 ·

A WINGÉD spark doth soar about,
I never met it near,
For lightning it is oft mistook
When nights are hot and sere.

Its twinkling travels it pursues
Above the haunts of men—
A speck of rapture first perceived
By feeling it is gone.

· 44 ·

I WATCHED the moon around the house
Until upon a pane
She stopped—a traveler's privilege—
For rest, and thereupon

I gazed, as at a stranger
The lady in the town
Doth think no incivility
To lift her glass upon.

But never stranger justified
The curiosity
Like mine, for not a foot nor hand
Nor formula had she,

But like a head a guillotine
Slid carelessly away,
Did independent amber
Sustain her in the sky;

Or like a stemless flower
Upheld in rolling air
By finer gravitations
Than bind philosopher.

No hunger had she, nor an inn
Her toilette to suffice,
Nor avocation, nor concern
For little mysteries

As harass us—like life and death
And afterward, or nay—
But seemed engrossed to absolute
With shining and the sky.

The privilege to scrutinize
Was scarce upon my eyes,
When with a silver practice
She vaulted out of gaze.

And next I met her on a cloud,
Myself too far below
To follow her superior road
Or its advantage blue.

· 45 ·

The road was lit with moon and star,
The trees were bright and still;
Descried I in the distant light
A traveler on a hill

To magic perpendiculars
Ascending, though terrene,
Unknown his shimmering ultimate,
But he indorsed the sheen.

· 46 ·

'Tis my first night beneath the sun
If I should spend it here;
Above him is too low a height
For his barometer

Who airs of expectation breathes
And takes the wind at prime,
But distance his delights confides
To those who visit him.

· 47 ·

How mighty the wind must feel morns,
Encamping on a thousand dawns,
Espousing each and spurning all,
Then soaring to his turret tall!

How pompous the wind must feel noons,
Stepping to incorporeal tunes,
Correcting errors of the sky
And skirmishing with scenery!

How lonesome the wind must feel nights
When people have put out the lights,
And everything that has an inn
Closes his shutter and goes in![1]

[1] In a different version the order of the stanzas is reversed.

· 48 ·

A NIGHT there lay the days between,
The day that was before
And day that was behind were one,
And now 'twas night was here—

Slow night, that must be watched away
As grains upon a shore,
Too imperceptible to note
Till it be night no more.

The Round Year

· 49 ·

THE snow that never drifts—
The transient, fragrant snow
That comes a single time a year—
Is softly driving now;

So thorough in the tree
At night beneath the star
That it was February's self
Experience would swear;

Like winter as a face
We stern and former knew
Repaired of all but loneliness
By nature's alibi.

Were every storm so spice,
The value could not be;
We buy with contrast—pang is good
As near as memory.

· 50 ·

THE notice that is called the spring
Is but a month from here;
Put up, my heart, thy hoary work
And take a rosy chair.

Not any house the flowers keep,
The birds enamor care,
Our salary the longest day
Is nothing but a bier.

· 51 ·

I SUPPOSE the time will come—
Aid it in the coming!—
When the bird will crowd the tree
And the bee be booming.

I suppose the time will come—
Hinder it a little—
When the corn in silk will dress
And in chintz the apple.

I believe the day will be
When the jay will giggle
At his new white house, the earth—
That too halt a little!

· 52 ·

SPRING is the period
Express from God.
Among the other seasons
Himself abide,

But during March and April
None stir abroad
Without a cordial interview
With God.

· 53 ·

I CANNOT meet the spring unmoved,
I feel the old desire—
A hurry with a lingering mixed,
A warrant to be fair,

A competition in my sense
With something hid in her,
And as she vanishes, remorse
I saw no more of her.

· 54 ·

HAD we our senses—though perhaps
'Tis well they're not at home,
So intimate with madness
'Tis liable with them—

Had we the eyes within our heads—
How well that we are blind!—
We could not look upon the earth
So utterly unmoved.

· 55 ·

SUMMER we all have seen,
A few of us believed;
A few, the more aspiring,
Unquestionably loved.

But summer does not care,
She goes her spacious way
As eligible as the moon
To our extremity.

Created to adore,
The affluence bestowed
Unknown as to an ecstasy
The embryo endowed.

· 56 ·

Someone prepared this mighty show
To which without a ticket go
The nations and the days,

Displayed before the simplest door
That all may witness it and more,
The pomp of summer days.

· 57 ·

A soft sea washed around the house,
A sea of summer air,
And rose and fell the magic planks
That sailed without a care.

For captain was the butterfly,
For helmsman was the bee,
And an entire universe
For the delighted crew.

· 58 ·

These fevered days to take them to the forest,
Where waters cool around the mosses crawl,
And shade is all that devastates the stillness,
Seems it sometimes this would be all.

· 59 ·

The summer that we did not prize,
Her treasurers were so easy,
Instructs us by departure now;
And recognition lazy

Bestirs itself, puts on its coat,
And scans with fatal promptness
For trains that moment out of sight,
Unconscious of his smartness.

· 60 ·

THERE comes a warning like a spy—
A shorter breath of day,
A stealing that is not a stealth,
A symptom that is not a sound,
  And summer is away.

· 61 ·

WITHOUT a smile, without a throe,
Do summer's soft assemblies go
  To their entrancing end,
Unknown, for all the times we met,
Estranged, however intimate—
  What a dissembling friend!

· 62 ·

SEPTEMBER's baccalaureate
A combination is
Of crickets, crows, and retrospects,
And a dissembling breeze

That hints, without assuming,
An innuendo sere
That makes the heart put up its fun
And turn philosopher.[2]

[2] Published in *The Youth's Companion*, September 29, 1892.

· 63 ·

Did we abolish frost
The summer would not cease.
If seasons perish or prevail
Is optional with us.

· 64 ·

The pungent atom in the air
Admits of no debate.
All that is named of summer days
Relinquished our estate

For what department of delight
As positive are we
As limit of dominion
Or dams of ecstasy.

· 65 ·

The name of it is autumn,
The hue of it is blood,
An artery upon the hill,
A vein along the road,

Great globules in the alleys,
And oh, the shower of stain
When winds upset the basin
And spill the scarlet rain!

It sprinkles bonnets far below,
It gathers ruddy pools,
Then eddies like a rose away
Upon vermilion wheels.[3]

[3] This poem was published in *The Youth's Companion*, September 8, 1892, with a different last line, "And leaves me with the hills."

· 66 ·

THE products of my farm are these,
Sufficient for my own
And here and there a benefit
Unto a neighbor's bin.

With us 'tis harvest all the year,
For when the frosts begin,
We just reverse the zodiac
And fetch the acres in.

· 67 ·

TWICE had summer her fair verdure
Proffered to the plain;
Twice a winter's silver fracture
On the rivers been;

Two full autumns for the squirrel
Bounteous prepared.
Nature! Hadst thou not a berry
For thy wandering bird?

· 68 ·

THERE is a June when corn is cut
And roses in the seed,
A summer briefer than the first
But tenderer indeed

As should a face, supposed the grave's,
Emerge a single noon
In the vermilion that it wore,
Affect us, and return.

Two seasons, it is said, exist:
The summer of the just,
And this of ours, diversified
With prospect and with frost.

May not our second with its first
So infinite compare
That we but recollect the one
The other to adore?

· 69 ·

SUMMER has two beginnings,
Beginning once in June,
Beginning in October
Affectingly again,

Without perhaps the riot,
But graphicker for grace—
As finer is a going
Than a remaining face—

Departing then forever,
Forever until May.
Forever is deciduous
Except to those who die.

· 70 ·

THE day grew small, surrounded tight
By early, stooping night,
The afternoon in evening deep
Its yellow shortness dropped,

The winds went out their martial ways,
The leaves obtained excuse,
November hung his granite hat
Upon a nail of plush.

· 71 ·

A CHILLY peace infests the grass,
The sun respectful lies,
Not any trance of industry
These shadows scrutinize

Whose allies go no more abroad
For service or for glee,
Though all mankind do anchor here
From whatsoever sea.

· 72 ·

IT SIFTS from leaden sieves,
It powders all the wood,
It fills with alabaster wool
The wrinkles of the road.

It scatters like the birds,
Condenses like a flock,
Like juggler's figures situates
Upon a baseless arc.

It traverses, yet halts,
Disperses while it stays,
Then curls itself in Capricorn
Denying that it was.[4]

[4] Several versions of this poem in handwriting of different periods have the same opening stanza. One version was published in *Poems*, Second Series, 1891, p. 174.

· 73 ·

GLASS was the street, in tinsel peril
Tree and traveler stood;
Filled was the air with merry venture,
Hearty with boys the road;

Shot the lithe sleds like shod vibrations
Emphasized and gone—
It is the past's supreme italic
Makes the present mean.

· 74 ·

WINTER is good, his hoar delights
Italic flavor yield
To intellects inebriate
With summer or the world;

Generic as a quarry,
And hearty as a rose,
Invited with asperity,
But welcome when he goes.

My Pageantry

· 75 ·

ALL these my banners be!
I sow my pageantry
  In May.
It rises train by train,
Then sleeps in state again,
My chancel all the plain
  Today.

· 76 ·

TO LOSE, if one can find again,
To miss, if one shall meet,
The burglar cannot rob then,
The broker cannot cheat.

So build the hillocks gaily
Thou little spade of mine,
Leaving nooks for daisy
And for columbine.

You and I the secret
Of the crocus know,
Let us chant it softly,
"*There* is no more snow!"

· 77 ·

TO HIM who keeps an orchis' heart,
The swamps are pink with June.[5]

[5] Emily may have thought of 75, 76, and 77 as parts of one poem, since she wrote them all on one page without her usual marks of separation.

· 78 ·

BLOOM is result. To meet a flower
And casually glance
Would cause one scarcely to suspect
The minor circumstance

Assisting in the bright affair
So intricately done,
Then offered as a butterfly
To the meridian.

To pack the bud, oppose the worm,
Obtain its right of dew,
Adjust the heat, elude the wind,
Escape the prowling bee,

Great nature not to disappoint
Awaiting her that day—
To be a flower is profound
Responsibility!

· 79 ·

ABSENT place, an April day,
Daffodils a-blow;
Homesick curiosity
To the soul that snow-
Drift may block within it
Deeper than without;
Daffodil delight but
Whom it duplicate.

· 80 ·

FLOWERS—well, if anybody
Can the ecstasy define,
Half a transport, half a trouble,
With which flowers humble men,
Anybody find the fountain
From which floods so contra flow,
I will give him all the daisies
Which upon the hillside blow.

Too much pathos in their faces
For a simple breast like mine.
Butterflies from San Domingo
Cruising round the purple line
Have a system of aesthetics
Far superior to mine.

· 81 ·

BAFFLED for just a day or two,
Embarrassed, not afraid,
Encounter in my garden
An unexpected maid;

She beckons and the woods start,
She nods and all begin—
Surely such a country
I was never in!

· 82 ·

THEY ask but our delight,
The darlings of the soil,
And grant us all their countenance
For a penurious smile.

· 83 ·

Nobody knows this little rose,
It might a pilgrim be
Did I not take it from the ways
And lift it up to thee.

Only a bee will miss it,
Only a butterfly,
Hastening from far journey
On its breast to lie.

Only a bird will wonder,
Only a breeze will sigh—
Ah, little rose, how easy
For such as thee to die![6]

· 84 ·

Garlands for queens may be,
Laurels for rare degree
  Of soul or sword.
Ah, but remembering me,
Ah, but remembering thee,
Nature in chivalry,
Nature in charity,
Nature in equity,
  The rose ordained.

[6] Published in *The Youth's Companion*, December 24, 1891.

· 85 ·

ARTISTS wrestled here!
Lo, a tint cashmere!
Lo, a rose!
Student of the year,
For the easel here
Say repose!

· 86 ·

HEREIN a blossom lies,
A sepulchre between,
Cross it and overcome the bee;
Remain—'tis but a rind.

· 87 ·

HERE, where the daisies fit my head,
'Tis easiest to lie,
And every grass that plays outside
Is sorry, some, for me.

Where I am not afraid to go
I may confide my flower;
Who was not enemy of me
Will gentle be to her,

Nor separate herself and me
By distances become—
A single bloom we constitute,
Departed or at home.

· 88 ·

THEY have a little odor that to me
Is metre, nay, 'tis melody,
And spiciest at fading, indicate
A habit of a laureate.[7]

· 89 ·

NATURE affects to be sedate
Upon occasion grand,
But let our observation halt,
Her practices extend

To necromancy and the trades,
Remote to understand—
Behold our spacious citizen
Unto a juggler turned!

· 90 ·

TO HER derided home
A weed of summer came;
She did not know her station low
Nor ignominy's name

Bestowed a summer long
Upon a fameless flower,
Then swept as lightly from disdain
As lady from her bower.

[7] In *Ancestors' Brocades,* p. 36, I have used "poesy," Emily's alternative reading for "melody."

The dandelion's shield
Is valid as a star;
Leontodon's escutcheon
Sustains her anywhere.[8]

· 91 ·

Of nature I shall have enough
When I have entered these,
Entitled to a bumblebee's
Familiarities.

· 92 ·

The veins of other flowers
The scarlet flowers are
Till nature leisure has for terms
As "branch" and "jugular."

We pass and she abides;
We conjugate her skill
While she creates and federates
Without a syllable.

· 93 ·

The good will of a flower
The man who would possess
Must first present certificate
Of minted holiness.

[8] In an earlier copy of this poem the third stanza reads:

Of bliss the codes are few,
As Jesus cites of Him,
"Come unto me," the moiety
That wafts the seraphim.

· 94 ·

I SEND you a decrepit flower
That nature sent to me
At parting; she was going south
And I designed to stay.

Her motive for the souvenir,
If sentiment for me
Or circumstance prudential,
Withheld invincibly.

· 95 ·

WHEN I count the seeds
That are sown beneath
To bloom so by and by;
When I con the people
Lain so low
To be received as high;

When I believe the garden
Mortal shall not see,
Pick by faith its blossom
And avoid its bee,
I can spare this summer
Unreluctantly.

· 96 ·

I HAD some things that I called mine,
And God, that He called His,
Till recently a rival claim
Disturbed these amities;

The property, my garden,
Which having sown with care,
He claims the pretty acre
And sends a bailiff there.

The station of the parties
Forbids publicity,
But justice is sublimer
Than arms or pedigree.

I'll institute an action—
I'll vindicate the law!
Jove, choose your counsel,
I retain Shaw![9]

· 97 ·

THE frost was never seen;
If met, too rapid passed,
Or in too unsubstantial team.
The flowers notice first

A stranger hovering round,
A symptom of alarm
In villages remotely set,
But search effaces him

Till some retrieveless night,
Our vigilance at waste,
The garden gets the only shot
That never could be traced.

Unproved is much we know,
Unknown the worst we fear,
Of strangers is the earth the inn,
Of secrets is the air.

"A man who used to dig for her—a day laborer." M. L. T.

To analyze perhaps
A Philip would prefer,
But labor vaster than myself
I find it, to infer.

· 98 ·

THE frost of death was on the pane.
"Protect your flower," said he.
Like sailors fighting with a leak
We fought mortality.

One passive flower we held to sea,
To mountain, to the sun,
Yet even on his scarlet shelf
To crawl the frost begun.

We pried him back. Ourselves we wedged
Himself and her between,
But easy as a narrow snake
He forked his way along

Till all her helpless beauty bent,
And then our wrath begun!
We hunted him to his ravine,
We chased him to his den,

We hated death and hated life,
And nowhere was to go.
The sea and continent there is
A larger, it is woe!

· 99 ·

LIKE time's appointed wrinkle
On a beloved face
We clutch the grace the tighter
Though we resent the crease.

The frost, himself so comely,
Dishevels every prime,
Asserting from his prism
That none can punish him.

· 100 ·

THE worthlessness of earthly things
The ditty is that nature sings
And then enforces their delight
Till rectitude is suffocate.

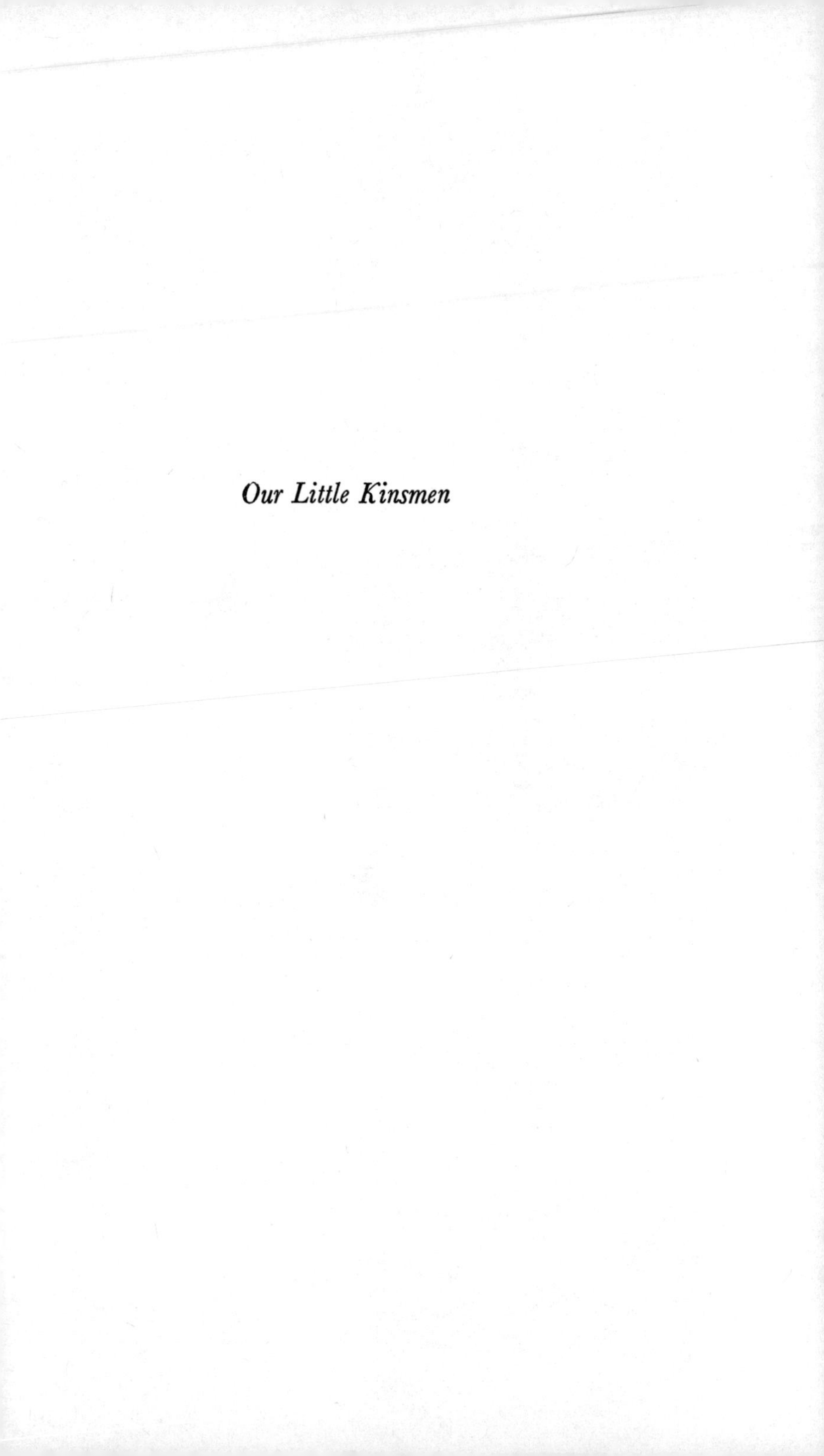

Our Little Kinsmen

· 101 ·

OUR little kinsmen after rain
In plenty may be seen,
A pink and pulpy multitude
The tepid ground upon;

A needless life it seemed to me
Until a little bird
As to a hospitality
Advanced and breakfasted.

As I of he, so God of me,
I pondered, may have judged,
And left the little angleworm
With modesties enlarged.

· 102 ·

HIS mansion in the pool
The frog forsakes.
He rises on a log
And statements makes.

His auditors two worlds
Deducting me,
The orator of April
Is hoarse today.

His mittens at his feet
No hand hath he,
His eloquence a bubble
As fame should be.

Applaud him, to discover
To your chagrin
Demosthenes has vanished
In forums green.

· 103 ·

It is a lonesome glee,
Yet sanctifies the mind
With fair association,
Remote upon the wind

A bird to overhear,
Delight without a cause,
Arrestless as invisible,
A matter of the skies.

· 104 ·

These strangers in a foreign world
Protection asked of me;
Befriend them, lest yourself in heaven
Be found a refugee.

· 105 ·

Cosmopolites without a plea
Alight in every land—
The compliments of paradise
From those within my hand—

Their dappled journey to themselves
A compensation gay.
"Knock and it shall be opened"
Is their theology.

· 106 ·

Touch lightly nature's sweet guitar
Unless thou know'st the tune,
Or every bird will point at thee
That wert a bard too soon.

· 107 ·

One joy of so much anguish
Sweet nature has for me,
I shun it as I do despair
Or dear iniquity.

Why birds, a summer morning
Before the quick of day,
Should stab my ravished spirit
With dirks of melody,

Is part of an inquiry
That will receive reply
When flesh and spirit sunder
In death's immediately!

· 108 ·

After all birds have been investigated and laid aside,
Nature imparts the little bluebird, assured
Her conscientious voice will soar unmoved
Above ostensible vicissitude.

First at the March, competing with the wind,
Her gallant note exalts us like a friend,
Last to adhere when summer swerves away,
Fortitude stanched with melody.[10]

[10] A version of this poem was printed in *The New England Quarterly*, April, 1932. One variant of the last two lines had previously appeared in *Letters*, 1894, p. 222.

· 109 ·

No BOBOLINK reverse his singing
When the only tree
Ever he minded occupying
By the farmer be.

Close to the core his spacious future,
Best horizon gone.
Brave bobolink, whose music be
His only anodyne!

· 110 ·

THE way to know the bobolink
From every other bird
Precisely as the joy of him
Obliged to be inferred:

Of impudent habiliment
Attired to defy,
Impertinence subordinate
At times to majesty;

Of sentiments seditious,
Amenable to law
As heresies of transport
Or Puck's apostasy;

Extrinsic to attention,
Too intimate with joy,
He compliments existence
Until allured away

By seasons, or his children
Adult and urgent grown,
Or unforeseen aggrandizement,
Or possibly renown,

By contrast certifying
The bird of birds is gone—
How nullified the meadow,
Her sorcerer withdrawn!

· 111 ·

The bobolink is gone,
The rowdy of the meadow,
And no one swaggers now but me;
The Presbyterian birds
Can now resume the meeting
He gaily interrupted
That overflowing day
When, opening the Sabbath
In their afflictive way,
He swung upon the decalogue
And shouted, "Let us pray!"

· 112 ·

I was a phebe, nothing more,
A phebe, nothing less;
The little note that others dropped
I fitted into place.

I dwelt too low that any seek,
Too shy that any blame;
A phebe makes a little print
Upon the floors of fame.

· 113 ·

A SPARROW took a slice of twig
And thought it very nice,
I think, because his empty plate
Was handed nature twice.

Invigorated fully,
Turned easy in the sky
As a familiar saddle
And rode immensity.

· 114 ·

THE robin is a troubadour
In humble circumstances—
The guests of perspicacity
A fugitive renown.

· 115 ·

YOU'LL know her by her foot.
The smallest gamboge hand
With fingers where the toes should be
Would more affront the sand

Than this quaint creature's boot,
Adjusted by a stem
Without a button, I could vouch,
Unto a velvet limb.

You'll know her by her vest,
Tight-fitting, orange-brown,
Inside a jacket duller
She wore when she was born.

Her cap is small and snug,
Constructed for the winds;
She'd pass for barehead short way off,
But as she closer stands

So finer 'tis than wool
You cannot feel the seam,
Nor is it clasped unto of band,
Nor has it any brim.

You'll know her by her voice,
At first a doubtful tone,
A sweet endeavor, but as March
To April hurries on,

She squanders on your ear
Such arguments of pearl,
You beg the robin in your brain
To keep the other still.

· 116 ·

THE robin for the crumb
Returns no syllable,
But long records the lady's name
In silver chronicle.

· 117 ·

SHE sights a bird, she chuckles,
She flattens, then she crawls,
She runs without the look of feet,
Her eyes increase to balls,

Her jaws stir, twitching, hungry,
Her teeth can hardly stand,
She leaps—but robin leaped the first!
Ah, pussy of the sand,

The hopes so juicy ripening
You almost bathed your tongue
When bliss disclosed a hundred wings
And fled with every one!

· 118 ·

His bill is locked, his eye estranged,
His feathers wilted low,
The claws that clung, like lifeless gloves
Indifferent hanging now;

The joy that in his happy throat
Was waiting to be poured,
Gored through and through with death. To be
Assassin of a bird

Resembles to my outraged mind
The firing in heaven
On angels, squandering for you
Their miracles of tune.

· 119 ·

A rat surrendered here
A brief career of cheer
And fraud and fear.

Of ignominy's due
Let all addicted to
Beware.

The most obliging trap
Its tendency to snap
Cannot resist.

Temptation is the friend
Repugnantly resigned
At last.

· 120 ·

The most important population
Unnoticed dwell;
They have a heaven each minute,
Not any hell;

Their names, unless you know them,
'Twere useless tell;
Of bumblebees and other nations
The grass is full.

· 121 ·

Bee, I'm expecting you!
Was saying yesterday
To somebody you know
That you were due.

The frogs got home last week,
Are settled and at work,
Birds mostly back,
The clover warm and thick.

You'll get my letter by
The seventeenth; reply,
Or better, be with me.
Yours,
Fly.

· 122 ·

BEES are black with gilt surcingles,
Buccaneers of buzz,
Ride abroad in ostentation
And subsist on fuzz,

Fuzz ordained, not fuzz contingent,
Marrows of the hill,
Jugs a universe's fracture
Could not jar or spill.

· 123 ·

THE pedigree of honey
Does not concern the bee,
Nor lineage of ecstasy
Delay the butterfly

On spangled journeys to the peak
Of some perceiveless thing,
The right of way to Tripoli
A more essential thing.[11]

· 124 ·

A SINGLE clover plank
Was all that saved a bee—
A bee I personally knew—
From sinking in the sky;

'Twixt firmament above,
And firmament below,
The billows of circumference
Were sweeping him away;

[11] The first two lines of this poem introduced a quatrain published in *Poems*, 1890, p. 73.

The idly swaying plank,
Responsible to naught,
A sudden freight of wind took on
And bumblebee was not.

This harrowing event
Transpiring in the grass
Did not so much as wring from him
A wandering "Alas!"

· 125 ·

Of silken speech and specious shoe,
A traitor is the bee,
His service to the newest grace
Present continually;

His suit a chance, his troth a term
Protracted as the breeze,
Continual ban propoundeth he,
Continual divorce.

· 126 ·

Upon a lilac sea
To toss incessantly
  His plush alarm,
Who fleeing from the spring,
The spring avenging fling
  To dooms of balm.

· 127 ·

A BEE his burnished carriage
Drove boldly to a rose,
Combinedly alighting,
Himself his equipage.

The rose received his visit
With frank tranquillity,
Withholding not a crescent
To his cupidity.

Their moment consummated,
Remained for him to flee,
Remained for her of rapture
But the humility.

· 128 ·

LEAST bee that brew a honey's weight
The summer multiply,
Content her smallest fraction help
The amber quantity.

· 129 ·

HIS oriental heresies
Exhilarate the bee,
And filling all the earth and air
With gay apostasy,

Fatigued at last, a clover plain
Allures his jaded eye,
That lowly breast where butterflies
Have felt it meet to die.

Intoxicated with the peace
Surpassing revelry,
He spends the evening of his days
In luscious revery,

Recounting nectars he has known
And attars that have failed,
And honeys, if his life be spared,
He hungers to attain.

· 130 ·

THESE are the nights that beetles love!
From eminence remote
Drives ponderous perpendicular
His figure intimate.

The terror of the children,
The jeopardy of men,
Depositing his thunder
He hoists abroad again.

A bomb upon the ceiling
Is an improving thing,
It keeps the nerves progressive,
Conjecture flourishing.

Too dear the summer evening
Without discreet alarm
Supplied by entomology
With its remaining charm!

· 131 ·

Two butterflies went out at noon
And waltzed upon a farm,
And then espied circumference
And caught a ride with him;

Then lost themselves and found themselves
In eddies of the sun,
Till rapture missed her footing
And both were wrecked in noon.

To all surviving butterflies
Be this biography,
Example, and monition
To entomology.[12]

· 132 ·

The butterfly's Numidian gown
With spots of burnish roasted on
  Is proof against the sun,
Yet prone to shut its dappled fan,
And languid on a clover lean
  As if it were undone.

· 133 ·

A moth the hue of this
Haunts candles in Brazil.
Nature's experience would make
Our reddest second pale.
Nature is fond, I sometimes think,
Of trinkets as a girl.

[12] A poem with the same first line was published in *Poems*, Second Series, 1891, p. 133.

· 134 ·

From his slim palace in the dust
He relegates the realm,
More loyal for the exody
That has befallen him.

· 135 ·

A burdock twitched my gown,
Not burdock's blame, but mine
Who went too near
The burdock's den.

A bog affronts my shoe,
What else have bogs to do,
The only art they know
The splashing men?

'Tis minnows should despise;
An elephant's calm eyes
Look further on.

· 136 ·

Those cattle smaller than a bee
That herd upon the eye,
Whose pasture is the passing crumb—
Those cattle are the fly.

Of barns for winter ignorant,
Extemporaneous stalls
They found, to our abhorrence,
On eligible walls,

Reserving the presumption
To suddenly descend
And gallop on the furniture
Or odiouser offend.

Of their peculiar calling
Unqualified to judge,
To nature we remand them
To justify or scourge.

· 137 ·

THE judge is like the owl
I've heard my father tell,
And owls do build in oaks,
So here's an amber sill

That slanted in my path
When going to the barn,
And if it serve you for a house
Itself is not in vain.

About the price, 'tis small,
I only ask a tune
At midnight—let the owl select
His favorite refrain.

· 138 ·

THE spider holds a silver ball
In unperceivéd hands
And dancing softly to himself
His yarn of pearl unwinds.

He plies from naught to naught
In unsubstantial trade,
Supplants our tapestries with his
In half the period—

An hour to rear supreme
His theories of light,
Then dangle from the housewife's broom,
His sophistries forgot.

· 139 ·

THE earth has many keys.
Where melody is not
Is the unknown peninsula.
Beauty is nature's fact.

But witness for her land,
And witness for her sea,
The cricket is her utmost
Of elegy to me.

· 140 ·

ITS little ether hood
Doth sit upon its head—
The millinery supple
Of the sagacious God—

Till when it slip away
A nothing at a time,
And dandelion's drama
Expires in a stem.

· 141 ·

THE jay his castanet has struck,
Put on your muff for winter,
The tippet that ignores his voice
Is infidel to nature.

Of swarthy days he is the close,
His lotus is a chestnut,
The cricket is a sable line—
No more from yours at present.

· 142 ·

FOUR trees upon a solitary acre
Without design
Or order or apparent action
Maintain.

The sun upon a morning meets them,
The wind;
No nearer neighbor have they
But God.

The acre gives them place,
They, him, attention of passer-by—
Of shadow, or of squirrel, haply,
Or boy.

What deed is theirs unto the general nature,
What plan
They severally promote or hinder,
Unknown.

· 143 ·

An antiquated tree
Is cherished by the crow
Because that junior foliage
Is disrespectful now

To venerable birds
Whose corporation coat
Would decorate oblivion's
Most pompous consulate.

· 144 ·

How fits his umber coat
The tailor of the nut,
Combined without a seam
Like raiment of a dream?

Who spun the auburn cloth?
Computed how the girth?
The chestnut agéd grows
In those primeval clothes.

We know that we are wise,
Accomplished in surprise,
Yet by this countryman,
This nature, how undone!

· 145 ·

A saucer holds a cup
In sordid human life,
But in a squirrel's estimate
A saucer holds a loaf.

A table of a tree
Demands the little king,
And every breeze that run along
His dining-room doth swing.

His cutlery he keeps
Between his russet lips,
To see it flashing when he dines
Do Birmingham eclipse.

· 146 ·

CONVICTED could we be
Of our minutiae,
The smallest citizen that flies
Has more integrity.

· 147 ·

'TIS customary as we part
A trinket to confer;
It helps to stimulate the faith
When lovers be afar.

'Tis various as the various taste.
Clematis, journeying far,
Presents me with a single curl
Of her electric hair.

· 148 ·

THE gentian has a parched corolla
Like azure dried,
'Tis nature's buoyant juices
Beatified,
Without a vaunt or sheen,
As casual as rain,
And as benign.

When most is past it comes,
Nor isolate it seems,
Its bond its friend;
To fill its fringed career
And aid an agéd year
Abundant end.

Its lot were it forgot
This truth declare:
Fidelity is gain
Creation o'er.

· 149 ·

I THOUGHT that nature was enough
Till human nature came,
But that the other did absorb
As firmament a flame.

Of human nature just aware
There added the divine
Brief struggle for capacity.
The power to contain

Is always as the contents,
But give a giant room
And you will lodge a giant
And not a lesser man.

Once a Child

· 150 ·

IT TROUBLED me as once I was,
For I was once a child,
Deciding how an atom fell
And yet the heavens held.

The heavens weighed the most by far,
Yet blue and solid stood
Without a bolt that I could prove;
Would giants understand?

Life set me larger problems,
Some I shall keep to solve
Till algebra is easier
Or simpler proved above.

Then too be comprehended
What sorer puzzled me,
Why heaven did not break away
And tumble blue on me.

151 ·

IT WAS given to me by the gods
When I was a little girl.
They give us presents most you know
When we are new and small.

I kept it in my hand,
I never put it down,
I did not dare to eat or sleep
For fear it would be gone.

I heard such words as "rich,"
When hurrying to school,
From lips at corners of the streets,
And wrestled with a smile.

Rich! 'Twas myself was rich!
To take the name of gold,
And gold to own in solid bars—
The difference made me bold.

· 152 ·

The parasol is the umbrella's daughter
And associates with a fan,
While her father abuts the tempest
And abridges the rain.

The former assists a siren
In her serene display;
But the latter, her sire, is honored
And borrowed to this day.

· 153 ·

The angle of a landscape
That every time I wake
Between my curtain and the wall
Upon an ample crack

Like a Venetian, waiting,
Accosts my open eye,
Is just a bough of apples
Held slanting in the sky,

The pattern of a chimney,
The forehead of a hill,
Sometimes a vane's forefinger—
But that's occasional.

The seasons shift my picture.
Upon my emerald bough
I wake to find no emeralds;
Then diamonds which the snow

From polar caskets fetched me.
The chimney and the hill
And just the steeple's finger,
These never stir at all.

· 154 ·

WHAT is paradise? Who live there?
Are they farmers? Do they hoe?
Do they know that this is Amherst,
And that I am coming, too?

Do they wear new shoes in Eden?
Is it always pleasant there?
Won't they scold us when we're homesick,
Or tell God how cross we are?

You are sure there's such a person
As a Father in the sky,
So if I get lost there, ever,
Or do what the nurse calls "die,"

I shan't walk the jasper barefoot,
Ransomed folks won't laugh at me?
Maybe Eden ain't so lonesome
As New England used to be!

· 155 ·

We don't cry, Tim and I,
We are far too grand!
But we bolt the door tight
To prevent a friend.

Then we hide our brave face
Deep in our hand,
Not to cry, Tim and I,
We are far too grand!

Nor to dream, he and me,
Do we condescend,
We just shut our brown eye
To see to the end.

"Tim, see cottages,
But oh, so high!"
Then we shake, Tim and I,
And lest I cry

Tim reads a little hymn,
And we both pray.
"Please, Sir, I and Tim
Always lost the way!"

We must die by and by
Clergymen say,
Tim shall, if I do,
I too, if he.

How shall we arrange it,
Tim was so shy?
Take us simultaneous, Lord
I, Tim, and me!

· 156 ·

I MET a king this afternoon;
He had not on a crown, indeed
A little palm-leaf hat was all,
And he was barefoot I'm afraid.

But sure I am he ermine wore
Beneath his faded jacket's blue,
And sure I am the crest he bore
Within that jacket's pocket too.

For 'twas too stately for an earl,
A marquis would not go so grand,
'Twas possibly a czar petite,
A pope, or something of that kind!

If I must tell you, of a horse
My freckled monarch held the rein,
Doubtless an estimable beast
But not at all disposed to run.

And such a wagon! While I live
Dare I presume to see
Another such a vehicle
As then transported me!

Two other ragged princes
His royal state partook,
Doubtless the first excursion
These sovereigns ever took.

I question if the royal coach
Round which the footmen wait
Has the significance, on high,
Of this barefoot estate![12a]

[12a] Published in *The Youth's Companion,* May 18, 1893, page 256.

· 157 ·

A LITTLE dog that wags his tail
And knows no other joy,
Of such a little dog am I
Reminded by a boy

Who gambols all the living day
Without an earthly cause,
Because he is a little boy,
I honestly suppose.

The cat that in the corner dwells,
Her martial day forgot,
The mouse but a tradition now
Of her desireless lot,

Another class remind me
Who neither please nor play,
But not to make "a bit of noise"
Beseech each little boy.

· 158 ·

So I pull my stockings off,
Wading in the water
For the disobedience' sake;
Boy that lived for "or'ter"
Went to heaven perhaps at death,
And perhaps he didn't.
Moses wasn't fairly used—
Ananias wasn't.

· 159 ·

THE blackberry wears a thorn in his side,
But no man heard him cry;
He offers his berry just the same
To partridge and to boy.

He sometimes holds upon the fence,
Or struggles to a tree,
Or clasps a rock with both his hands,
But not for sympathy.

We tell a hurt to cool it;
This mourner to the sky
A little farther climbs instead—
Brave blackberry!

· 160 ·

ABRAHAM to kill him
Was distinctly told;
Isaac was an urchin,
Abraham was old.

Not a hesitation,
Abraham complied;
Flattered by obeisance,
Tyranny demurred.

Isaac to his children
Lived to tell the tale.
Moral: with a mastiff
Manners may prevail.

· 161 ·

OVER the fence strawberries grow;
Over the fence I could climb
If I tried, I know—
Berries are nice!

But if I stained my apron
God would certainly scold!
Oh, dear! I guess if He were a boy
He'd climb, if He could!

· 162 ·

HE TOLD a homely tale
And spotted it with tears;
Upon his infant face was set
The cicatrice of years.

All crumpled was the cheek
No other kiss had known
Than flake of snow divided with
The redbreast of the barn.

If mother in the grave,
Or father on the sea,
Or Father in the firmament,
Or brethren, had he,

If commonwealth below,
Or commonwealth above
Have missed a barefoot citizen,
I've ransomed it alive!

· 163 ·

TRUDGING to Eden, looking backward,
I met somebody's little boy,
Asked him his name, he lisped me, "Trotwood."
Lady, did he belong to thee?

Would it comfort to know I met him,
And that he didn't look afraid?
I couldn't weep, for so many smiling
New acquaintance this baby made.

· 164 ·

GOOD to hide and hear 'em hunt!
Better, to be found,
If one care to, that is,
The fox fits the hound.

Good to know and not tell,
Best to know and tell,
Can one find the rare ear
Not too dull.

· 165 ·

THIS dirty little heart
Is freely mine—
I won it with a bun—
A freckled shrine,

But eligibly fair
To him who sees
The visage of the soul
And not the knees.

· 166 ·

THE hills in purple syllables
The day's adventures tell
To little groups of continents
Just going home from school.

· 167 ·

THE lady feeds her little bird
At rarer intervals;
The little bird would not demur,
But meekly recognize

The gulf between the hand and her,
And crumbless and afar
And fainting, on her yellow knee
Fall softly and adore.

· 168 ·

MAMA never forgets her birds
Though in another tree;
She looks down just as often
And just as tenderly

As when her little mortal nest
With cunning care she wove.
If either of her "sparrows fall"
She "notices" above.[13]

[13] This poem was sent to Emily's young cousins, Louisa and Fanny Norcross, on the death of their mother, April 17, 1860.

· 169 ·

'Tis one by one the Father counts,
And then a tract between
Set cipherless to teach the eye
The value of its ten,

Until the peevish student
Acquire the quick of skill;
Then numerals are dowered back,
Adorning all the rule.

'Tis mostly slate and pencil
And darkness on the school
Distracts the children's fingers.
Still the Eternal Rule

Regards least cipher alike
With leader of the band,
And every separate urchin's sum
Is fitted to his hand.

· 170 ·

The beggar lad dies early.
It's somewhat in the cold,
And somewhat in the trudging feet,
And haply in the world—

The cruel, smiling, bowing world—
That took its cambric way,
Nor heard the timid cry for "Bread!
Sweet lady, charity!"

Among redeemèd children
If trudging feet may stand,
The barefoot time forgotten so,
The sleet, the bitter wind,

The childish hands that teased for pence
Lifted adoring then
To Him whom never ragged coat
Did supplicate in vain.

· 171 ·

WE DO not play on graves
Because there isn't room;
Besides, it isn't even,
It slants, and people come

And put a flower on it,
And hang their faces so,
We're fearing that their hearts will drop
And crush our pretty play.

And so we move as far
As enemies away,
Just looking round to see how far
It is, occasionally.

· 172 ·

RIBBONS of the year,
Multitude brocade,
Worn to nature's party once,
Then as flung aside

As a faded bead
Or a wrinkled pearl—
Who shall charge the vanity
Of the Maker's girl?

· 173 ·

MAKE me a picture of the sun
So I can hang it in my room
And make believe I'm getting warm
When others call it "day"!

Draw me a robin on a stem,
So I am hearing him I'll dream,
And when the orchards stop their tune
Put my pretense away.

Say if it's really warm at noon,
Whether it's buttercups that skim,
Or butterflies that bloom.
Then skip the frost upon the lea
And skip the russet on the tree—
Let's play those never come!

· 174 ·

Snow Flakes[14]

I COUNTED till they danced so
Their slippers leaped the town,
And then I took a pencil
To note the rebels down;

And then they grew so jolly
I did resign the prig,
And ten of my once stately toes
Are marshaled for a jig!

[14] Emily's title.

The Mob within the Heart

· 175 ·

THE mob within the heart
Police cannot suppress.
The riot given at the first
Is authorized as peace,

Not certified of scene
Or signified of sound,
But growing like a hurricane
In a congenial ground.

· 176 ·

'TIS true they shut me in the cold,
But then, themselves were warm
And could not know the feeling 'twas—
Forget it, Lord, of them!

Let not my witness hinder them
In heavenly esteem,
No paradise could be conferred
Through their belovéd blame.

The harm they did was short, and since
Myself who owe it do,
Forgive them even as myself,
Or else forgive not me!

· 177 ·

IT WOULD have starved a gnat
To dine so small as I,
And yet I was a living child
With food's necessity

Upon me like a claw.
I could no more remove
Than I could coax a leech away
Or make a dragon move.

Nor like the gnat had I
The privilege to fly
And seek a dinner for myself,
How mightier he than I!

Nor like himself the art
Upon the window pane
To gad my little being out
And not begin again.

· 178 ·

I CRIED at pity, not at pain.
I heard a woman say,
"Poor child," and something in her voice
Convicted me of me.

So long I fainted, to myself
It seemed the common way,
And health and laughter curious things
To look at, like a toy—

To sometimes hear "rich people" buy,
And see the parcel rolled
And carried, I supposed, to heaven
For children made of gold—

But not to touch or wish for
Or think of, with a sigh.

· 179 ·

I WAS the slightest in the house,
I took the smallest room,
At night, my little lamp and book
And one geranium,

So stationed I could catch the mint
That never ceased to fall,
And just my basket, let me think,
I'm sure that this was all.

I never spoke unless addressed,
And then 'twas brief and low,
I could not bear to live aloud
The racket shamed me so.

And if it had not been so far,
And anyone I knew
Were going, I had often thought
How noteless I could die.

· 180 ·

A LOSS of something ever felt I.
The first that I could recollect
Bereft I was, of what I knew not,
Too young that any should suspect

A mourner lurked among the children.
I notwithstanding stole about
As one bemoaning a dominion,
Itself the only prince cast out.

Elder today, a session wiser—
And fainter too, as wiseness is—
I find myself still softly searching
For my delinquent palaces,

And a suspicion like a finger
Touches my forehead now and then,
That I am looking oppositely
For the site of the kingdom of heaven.

· 181 ·

ALONE and in a circumstance
Reluctant to be told,
A spider on my reticence
Deliberately crawled,

And so much more at home than I
Immediately grew,
I felt myself the visitor
And hurriedly withdrew.

Revisiting my late abode
With articles of claim,
I found it quietly assumed
As a gymnasium

Where, tax asleep and title off,
The inmates of the air
Perpetual presumption took
As each were lawful heir.

If any strike me on the street
I can return the blow;
If any seize my property,
According to the law

The statute is my learnéd friend;
But what redress can be
For an offense nor here nor there,
So not in equity,

That larceny of time and mind,
The marrow of the day,
By spider—or forbid it, Lord,
That I should specify.

· 182 ·

I THINK the longest hour of all
Is when the cars have come
And we are waiting for the coach;
It seems as though the time,

Affronted that the joy was come,
Did block the gilded hands
And would not let the seconds by—
But slowest instant ends.

The pendulum begins to count
Like little scholars, loud,
The steps grow thicker in the hall,
The heart begins to crowd,

Then I, my timid service done,
Though service 'twas of love,
Take up my little violin
And further north remove.

· 183 ·

Myself can read the telegrams,
A letter chief to me,
The stocks' advance and retrograde
And what the markets say,

The weather, how the rains
In counties have begun,
'Tis news as null as nothing,
But sweeter so than none.

· 184 ·

Up life's hill with my little bundle,
If I prove it steep,
If a discouragement withhold me,
If my newest step

Older feel than the hope that prompted,
Spotless be from blame
Heart that proposed, as heart that accepted,
Homelessness for home.

· 185 ·

As the starved maelstrom laps the navies,
As the vulture, teased,
Forces the broods in lonely valleys,
As the tiger, eased

By but a crumb of blood, fasts scarlet
Till he meet a man,
Dainty adorned with veins and tissues,
And partakes—his tongue,

Cooled by the morsel for a moment,
Grows a fiercer thing
Till he esteem his dates and cocoa
A nutrition mean—

I, of a finer famine,
Deem my supper dry
For but a berry of Domingo
And a torrid eye.

· 186 ·

I TRIED to think a lonelier thing
Than any I had seen—
Some polar expiation,
An omen in the bone

Of death's tremendous nearness—
I probed retrieveless things
My duplicate to borrow.
A haggard comfort springs

From the belief that somewhere
Within the clutch of thought
There dwells one other creature
Of Heavenly Love forgot.

I plucked at our partition,
As one should pry the walls
Between himself and horror's twin
Within opposing cells.

I almost strove to clasp his hand,
Such luxury it grew
That as myself could pity him
Perhaps he pitied me.

· 187 ·

I MADE slow riches but my gain
Was steady as the sun,
And every night it numbered more
Than the preceding one.

All days I did not earn the same,
But my perceiveless gain
Inferred the less by growing than
The sum that it had grown.

· 188 ·

I CANNOT buy it, 'tis not sold,
There is no other in the world,
  Mine was the only one.

I was so happy I forgot
To shut the door and it went out
  And I am all alone.

If I could find it anywhere
I would not mind the journey there
  Though it took all my store.

But just to look it in the eye,
"Didst thou?" "Thou didst not mean," to say,
  Then turn my face away.

· 189 ·

Oh, honey of an hour,
I never knew thy power!
Prohibit me
Till my minutest dower,
My unfrequented flower,
Deserving be.

· 190 ·

So large my will,
The little that I may
Embarrasses
Like gentle infamy.

Affront to Him
For Whom the whole were small,
Affront to me
Who know His meed of all.

Earth at the best
Is but a scanty toy,
Bought, carried home
To immortality,

It looks so small
We chiefly wonder then
At our conceit
In purchasing.

· 191 ·

If all the griefs I am to have
Would only come today,
I am so happy I believe
They'd laugh and run away!

If all the joys I am to have
Would only come today,
They could not be so big as this
That happens to me now!

· 192 ·

A DRUNKARD cannot meet a cork
Without a revery;
And so, encountering a fly
This January day,

Jamaicas of remembrance stir
That send me reeling in—
The moderate drinker of delight
Does not deserve the spring.

Of juleps part are in the jug
And more are in the joy;
Your connoisseur in liquors
Consults the bumblebee.

· 193 ·

THE day she goes or day she stays
Are equally supreme;
Existence has a stated width,
Departed or at home.

· 194 ·

OURSELVES were wed one summer, dear,
Your vision was in June,
And when your little lifetime failed
I wearied, too, of mine.

And overtaken in the dark,
Where you had put me down,
By someone carrying a light,
I, too, received the sign.

'Tis true our futures different lay,
Your cottage faced the sun,
While oceans and the north did play
On every side of mine.

'Tis true your garden led the bloom,
For mine in frosts was sown,
And yet, one summer we were queens,
But you were crowned in June.

· 195 ·

So much summer me for showing
Illegitimate—
Would a smile's minute bestowing
Too importunate

To the lady with the guinea
Look, if she should know
Crumb of mine a robin's larder
Could suffice to stow?

· 196 ·

Precious to me she still shall be,
Though she forget the name I bear,
The fashion of the gown I wear,
The very color of my hair.

So like the meadows now I dared
To show a tress of theirs,
If haply she might not despise
A buttercup's array.

I know the whole obscures the part,
The fraction that appeased the heart
  Till numbers' empery,
Remembered as the milliner's flower
When summer's everlasting dower
  Confronts the dazzled bee.

· 197 ·

I'll clutch and clutch,
Next one might be the golden touch
Could take it.
Diamonds, wait!
I'm diving, just a little late,
But stars go slow for night.

I'll string you in fine necklace,
Tiaras make of some,
Wear you on hem,
Loop up a countess with you,
Make a diadem and mend my old one,
Count, hoard, then lose,
And doubt that you are mine,
To have the joy of feeling it again!

I'll show you at the court,
Bear you for ornament
Where women breathe,
That every sigh may lift you
Just as high as I!

And when I die,
In meek array display you,
Still to show how rich I go,
Lest skies impeach a wealth so wonderful
And banish me.

· 198 ·

LIKE eyes that looked on wastes,
Incredulous of aught
But blank—and stead, wilderness
Diversified by night—

Just infinite of naught
As far as it could see,
So looked the face I looked upon.
So looked itself on me.

I offered it no help
Because the cause was mine,
The misery a compact
As hopeless as divine.

Neither would be absolved,
Neither would be a queen
Without the other—therefore
We perish, though we reign.

· 199 ·

IT DID not surprise me,
So I said, or thought,
She will stir her pinions
And, the nest forgot,

Traverse broader forests,
Build in gayer boughs,
Breathe in ear more modern
God's old-fashioned vows.

This was but a birdling,
What and if it be
One within my bosom
Had departed me?

This was but a story,
What and if indeed
There were just such coffin
In the heart instead?

· 200 ·

Had I known that the first was the last
I should have kept it longer.
Had I known that the last was the first
I should have mixed it stronger.

Cup, it was your fault,
Lip was not the liar!
No, lip, it was yours,
Bliss was most to blame!

· 201 ·

How happy I was if I could forget
To remember how sad I am
Would be an easy adversity,
But the recollecting of bloom

Keeps making November difficult
Till I, who was almost bold,
Lose my way like a little child
And perish of the cold.

· 202 ·

Now I knew I lost her—
Not that she was gone,
But remoteness traveled
On her face and tongue.

Alien, though adjoining,
As a foreign race,
Traversed she though pausing
Latitudeless place.

Elements unaltered,
Universe the same,
But love's transmigration—
Somehow this had come.

Henceforth to remember
Nature took the day
I had paid so much for.
His is penury

Not who toils for freedom
Or for family,
But the restitution
Of idolatry.

· 203 ·

THAT distance was between us
That is not of mile or main;
The will it is that situates,
Equator never can.

· 204 ·

WHOEVER disenchants
A single human soul
By failure or irreverence
Is guilty of the whole.

As guileless as a bird,
As graphic as a star,
Till caviler insinuates
Things are not what they are.

· 205 ·

I CANNOT want it more,
I cannot want it less,
My human nature's fullest force
Expends itself on this.

And yet it nothing is
To him who easy owns,
Is worth itself or distance
He fathoms who obtains.

· 206 ·

A GREAT hope fell, you heard no noise,
The ruin was within.
Oh, cunning wreck that told no tale
And let no witness in!

The mind was built for mighty freight,
For dread occasion planned,
How often foundering at sea,
Ostensibly on land!

A not admitting of the wound
Until it grew so wide
That all my life had entered it
And there was room beside.

A closing of the simple lid
That opened to the sun
Until the sovereign Carpenter
Perpetual nail it down.

· 207 ·

HAD I not seen the sun
I could have borne the shade;
But light a newer wilderness
My wilderness has made.

· 208 ·

FINDING is the first act;
The second, loss;
Third, expedition for
The golden fleece;

Fourth, no discovery;
Fifth, no crew;
Finally, no golden fleece—
Jason sham too.

· 209 ·

I HAD the glory—that will do—
An honor thought can turn her to
  When lesser fames invite,
With one long "Nay," bliss' early shape
Deforming, dwindling, gulfing up
  Time's possibility.

· 210 ·

KNOWS how to forget!
But could it teach it?
Easiest of arts they say
When one learn how.

Dull hearts have died
In the acquisition,
Sacrifice for science
Is common though now.

I went to school
But was not wiser,
Globe did not teach it
Nor logarithm show.

"How to forget!"
Say, some philosopher!
Ah, to be erudite
Enough to know!

Is it in a book?
So, I could buy it.
Is it like a planet?
Telescopes would know.

If it be invention
It must have a patent.
Rabbi of the Wise Book,
Don't you know?

· 211 ·

I COULD not prove the years had feet,
Yet confident they run
Am I from symptoms that are past
And series that are done.

I find my feet have further goals,
I smile upon the aims
That felt so ample yesterday—
Today's have vaster claims.

I do not doubt the self I was
Was competent to me;
But something awkward in the fit
Proves that outgrown, I see.

· 212 ·

I KNEW that I had gained
And yet I knew not how;
By diminution it was not,
But discipline unto

A rigor unrelieved
Except by the content
Another bear its duplicate
In other continent.

· 213 ·

Art thou the thing I wanted?
Begone! My tooth has grown!
Affront a minor palate
That has not starved so long!

I tell thee while I famished
The mystery of food
Increased till I abjured it,
Subsisting since like God.

· 214 ·

Where bells no more affright the morn,
Where scrabble never comes,
Where very nimble gentlemen
Are forced to keep their rooms,

Where tired children placid sleep
Through centuries of noon—
This place is bliss, this town is heaven!
Please, Pater, pretty soon!

Oh, could we climb where Moses stood
And view the landscape o'er,
Not Father's bells, nor factories,
Could scare us any more!

· 215 ·

IF THOSE I loved were lost,
The crier's voice would tell me;
If those I loved were found,
The bells of Ghent would ring;

Did those I loved repose,
The daisy would impel me.
Philip when bewildered
Bore his riddle in!

· 216 ·

SHELLS from the coast mistaking,
I cherished them for all.
Happening in after ages
To entertain a pearl,

"Wherefore so late?" I murmured,
"My need of thee be done."
"Therefore," the pearl responded,
"My period begin."

· 217 ·

CONSULTING summer's clock,
But half the hours remain;
I ascertain it with a shock,
I shall not look again.

The second half of joy
Is shorter than the first.
The truth I do not dare to know
I muffle with a jest.

· 218 ·

THE life that tied too tight escapes
Will ever after run
With a prudential look behind
And specters of the rein.

The horse that scents the living grass
And sees the pastures smile
Will be retaken with a shot
If he is caught at all.

· 219 ·

OF PAUL and Silas it is said
They were in prison laid,
But when they went to take them out
They were not there instead.

Security the same insures
To our assaulted minds.
The staple must be optional
That an immortal binds.

· 220 ·

"ESCAPE" is such a thankful word!
I often in the night
Consider it unto myself,
No citadel in sight.

"Escape"—it is the basket
In which the heart is caught
When down some awful battlement
The rest of life is dropped.

'Tis not to sight the savior,
It is to be the saved;
And that is why I lay my head
Upon this trusty word.

· 221 ·

ESCAPING backward, to perceive
The sea upon our place;
Escaping forward, to confront
His glittering embrace;

Retreating up, a billow's height;
Retreating blinded down,
Our undermining feet to meet,
Instructs to the divine.

· 222 ·

WE LIKE a hairbreadth 'scape,
It tingles in the mind
Far after act or accident,
Like paragraphs of wind.

If we had ventured less,
The breeze were not so fine
That reaches to our utmost hair
Its tentacles divine.

· 223 ·

MY FRIEND attacks my friend,
Oh, battle picturesque!
Then I turn soldier too,
And he turns satirist.

How martial is this place!
Had I a mighty gun
I think I'd shoot the human race
And then to glory run!

· 224 ·

DEPRIVED of other banquet
I entertained myself,
At first a scant nutrition,
An insufficient loaf,

But grown by slender addings
To so esteemed a size
'Tis sumptuous enough for me,
And almost to suffice

A robin's hunger able.
Red pilgrim, he and I
A berry from our table
Reserve for charity.

· 225 ·

MY BEST acquaintances are those
With whom I spoke no word;
The stars that stated come to town
Esteemed me never rude

Although to their celestial call
I failed to make reply,
My constant reverential face
Sufficient courtesy.

· 226 ·

In thy long paradise of light
No moment will there be
When I shall long for earthly play
And mortal company.

· 227 ·

My wars are laid away in books.
I have one battle more,
A foe whom I have never seen
But oft has scanned me o'er

And hesitated me between
And others at my side,
But chose the best, neglecting me
Till all the rest have died.

How sweet if I am not forgot
By chums that passed away,
Since playmates at threescore and ten
Are such a scarcity!

· 228 ·

This me that walks and works must die
Some fair or stormy day;
Adversity if it may be,
Or wild prosperity.

The rumor's gate was shut so tight
Before my mind was born,
Not even a prognostic's push
Can make a dent thereon.

· 229 ·

Jesus, Thy crucifix
Enables Thee to guess
The smaller size!

Jesus, Thy second face
Mind Thee in paradise
Of ours!

· 230 ·

I heard as if I had no ear
Until a vital word
Came all the way from life to me,
And then I knew I heard.

I saw as if my eye were on
Another, till a thing—
And now I know 'twas light because
It fitted them—came in.

I dwelt as if myself were out,
My body but within,
Until a might detected me
And set my kernel in.

And spirit turned unto the dust,
"Old friend, thou knowest me,"
And time went out to tell the news
And met eternity.[15]

[15] In slightly different form the final stanza was used in the draft of a letter to Colonel Higginson.

· 231 ·

Some wretched creature, Savior, take
Who would exult to die,
And leave for thy sweet mercy's sake
Another hour to me!

Italic Faces

· 233 ·

THE hollows round his eager eyes
Were pages where to read
Pathetic histories, although
Himself had not complained,

Biography to all who passed
Of unobtrusive pain
Except for the italic face
Endured, unhelped, unknown.

· 234 ·

TELL as a marksman were forgotten,
Tell this day endures
Ruddy as that coeval apple
The tradition bears.

Fresh as mankind that humble story,
Though a statelier tale
Grown in the repetition hoary
Scarcely could prevail.

Tell had a son—the ones that knew it
Need not linger here;
Those who do not, to human nature
Will subscribe a tear.

Tell would not bare his head in presence
Of the ducal hat,
Threatened for that with death by Gessler,
Tyranny bethought

Make of his only boy a target—
That surpasses death.
Stolid to love's supreme entreaty,
Not forsook of faith,

Mercy of the Almighty begging,
Tell his arrow sent.
God it is said replies in person
When the cry is meant.

· 235 ·

ELIZABETH told Essex
That she could not forgive;
The clemency of Deity,
However, might survive.

That secondary succor
We trust that she partook
When suing, like her Essex,
For a reprieving look.

· 236 ·

WOLFE demanded during dying,
"Which controlled the day?"
"General, the British." "Easy,"
Answered Wolfe, "to die."

Montcalm, his opposing spirit,
Rendered with a smile;
"Sweet," said he, "my own surrender
Liberty's forestall."

· 237 ·

WHEN the astronomer stops seeking
For his Pleiad's face,
When the lone British lady[16]
Forsakes the Arctic race,

When to his covenant needle
The sailor doubting turns,
It will be amply early
To ask what treason means.

· 238 ·

THE Malay took the pearl,
Not I, the Earl;
I feared the sea too much,
Unsanctified to touch,

Praying that I might be
Worthy the destiny.
The swarthy fellow swam
And bore my jewel home—

Home to the hut. What lot
Had I the jewel got!
Borne on a dusky breast!
I had not deemed a vest
Of amber fit!

The Negro never knew
I wooed it too.
To gain or be undone
Alike to him, one.

[16] Lady Jane, widow of Sir John Franklin, British naval hero lost in the Arctic in 1845, for years kept sending expeditions in search of him.

· 239 ·

A FADED boy in sallow clothes
Who drove a lonesome cow
To pastures of oblivion—
A statesman's embryo.

The boys that whistled are extinct,
The cows that fed and thanked,
Remanded to a ballad's barn
Or clover's retrospect.

· 240 ·

His mind like fabrics of the east
Displayed to the despair
Of everyone but here and there
An humble purchaser.

For though his price was not of gold
More arduous there is;
That one should comprehend the worth
Was all the price there was.

· 241 ·

His heart was darker than the starless night,
For that there is a morn,
But in this black receptacle
Can be no bode of dawn.

· 242 ·

THE ditch is dear to the drunken man,
For is it not his bed,
His advocate, his edifice?
How safe his fallen head

In her disheveled sanctity!
Above him is the sky,
Oblivion enfolding him
With tender infamy.

· 243 ·

HE OUTSTRIPPED time with but a bout,
He outstripped stars and sun,
And then, unjaded, challenged God
In presence of the throne,

And He and he in mighty list
Unto this present run,
The larger glory for the less
A just sufficient ring.

· 244 ·

WE SHUN because we prize her face
Lest proof's ineffable disgrace
Our adoration stain.

· 245 ·

HER face was in a bed of hair
Like flowers in a plot,
Her hand was whiter than the sperm
That feeds the sacred light,

Her tongue more tender than the tune
That totters in the leaves—
Who hears may be incredulous,
Who witnesses, believes.

· 246 ·

UNWORTHY of her breast—
Though by that scathing test
  What soul survive?
By her exacting light
How counterfeit the white
  We chiefly have!

· 247 ·

THE pretty rain from those sweet eaves—
Her unintending eyes—
Took her own heart, including ours,
By innocent surprise;

The wrestle in her simple throat
To hold the feeling down
That vanquished her, defeated feat,
Was fervor's sudden crown.

· 248 ·

His voice decrepit was with joy,
Her words did totter so,
How old the news of love must be
To make lips elderly
That purled a moment since with glee!
Is it delight or woe
Or terror that do generate
This livid interview?

· 249 ·

Because he loves her we will pry
And see if she is fair,
What difference is on her face
From features others wear.

It will not harm her magic pace
That we so far behind
Her distances propitiate
As forests touch the wind,

Not hoping for his notice vast,
But nearer to adore.
'Tis glory's overtakelessness
That makes our running poor.

· 250 ·

Had we known the ton she bore
We had helped the terror,
But she straighter walked for freight,
So be hers the error.

· 251 ·

AN ANTIQUATED grace
Becomes that cherished face
  Better than prime,
Enjoining us to part,
We and our pouting heart,
  Good friends with time.

· 252 ·

A LITTLE snow was here and there
Disseminated in her hair;
Since she and I had met and played
Decade had gathered to decade.

But time had added, not obtained.
Impregnable the rose,
For summer too inscrutable
Too sumptuous for snows.

The Infinite Aurora

· 253 ·

Struck was I, nor yet by lightning.
Lightning lets away
Power to perceive his process
With vitality.

Maimed was I, yet not by venture,
Stone of stolid boy,
Nor a sportsman's ruthless pleasure—
Who mine enemy?

Robbed was I, yet met no bandit,
All my mansion torn,
Sun withdrawn to recognition,
Furthest shining done,

Yet was not the foe of any—
Not the smallest bird
In the nearest orchard dwelling
Be of me afraid.

Most I love the cause that slew me;
Often as I die
Its belovéd recognition
Holds a sun on me,

Best at setting, as is nature's,
Neither witnessed rise
Till the infinite aurora
In the other's eyes.

· 254 ·

I AM alive, I guess,
The branches on my hand
Are full of morning-glory,
And at my fingers' end

The carmine tingles warm,
And if I hold a glass
Across my mouth it blurs it—
Physician's proof of breath.

I am alive, because
I am not in a room—
The parlor commonly it is—
So visitors may come

And lean, and view it sidewise,
And add, "How cold it grew!"
And "Was it conscious when it stepped
In immortality?"

I am alive, because
I do not own a house
Entitled to myself precise,
And fitting no one else,

And marked my girlhood's name
So visitors may know
Which door is mine, and not mistake
And try another key.

How good to be alive!
How infinite to be
Alive twofold, the birth I had,
And this besides, in thee!

· 255 ·

ALWAYS mine! No more vacation!
Term of light this day begun!
Failless as the fair rotation
Of the seasons and the sun!

Old the grace but new the subjects,
Old indeed the east,
Yet upon his purple program
Every dawn is first.

· 256 ·

SPRING comes on the world,
I sight the Aprils,
Hueless to me until thou come,
As till the bee
Blossoms stand negative,
Touched to conditions by a hum.

· 257 ·

ALL that I do is in review
To his enamored mind;
I know his eye where'er I ply
Is staring close behind.

Not any port, not any pause
But he doth there preside—
What omnipresence lies in wait
For an impending bride!

· 258 ·

I THOUGHT the train would never come.
How slow the whistle sang!
I don't believe a peevish bird
So whimpered for the spring.

I taught my heart a hundred times
Precisely what to say—
Provoking lover, when you came
Its treatise flew away!

To hide my strategy, too late,
To wiser grow, too soon,
For miseries so halcyon
The happiness atone.

· 259 ·

AGAIN his voice is at the door,
I feel the old degree,
I hear him ask the servant
For such an one as me;

I take a flower as I go
My face to justify,
He never saw me in this life,
I might surprise his eye.

I cross the hall with mingled steps,
I silent pass the door,
I look on all this world contains—
Just his face—nothing more!

We talk in venture and in toss,
A kind of plummet strain,
Each sounding shyly just how deep
The other's foot had been.

We walk. I leave my dog behind.
A tender thoughtful moon
Goes with us just a little way
And then we are alone.

Alone—if angels are alone
First time they try the sky!
Alone—if those veiled faces be
We cannot count on high!

I'd give to live that hour again
The purple in my vein;
But he must count the drops himself—
My price for every stain!

· 260 ·

We learned the whole of love,
The alphabet, the words,
A chapter, then the mighty book—
Then revelation closed.

But in each other's eyes
An ignorance beheld
Diviner than the childhood's,
And each to each a child

Attempted to expound
What neither understood.
Alas, that wisdom is so large
And truth so manifold!

· 261 ·

SANG from the heart, Sire,
Dipped my beak in it.
If the tune drip too much,
Have a tint too red,

Pardon the cochineal,
Suffer the vermilion,
Death is the wealth
Of the poorest bird.

Bear with the ballad,
Awkward, faltering,
Death twists the strings—
Twasn't my blame—

Pause in your liturgies,
Wait your chorals
While I repeat
Your hallowed name.

· 262 ·

OH, SUMPTUOUS moment, slower go,
That I may gloat on thee!
'Twill never be the same to starve
Since I abundance see.

Which was to famish, then or now?
The difference of day
Ask him unto the gallows called
With morning in the sky!

· 263 ·

He was weak and I was strong, then,
So he let me lead him in.
I was weak and he was strong, then,
So I let him lead me home.

'Twasn't far, the door was near,
'Twasn't dark, for he went too,
'Twasn't loud, for he said naught,
That was all I cared to know.

Day knocked, and we must part,
Neither was strongest now,
He strove, and I strove too.
We didn't do it though!

· 264 ·

Let my first knowing be of thee
With morning's warming light,
And my first fearing, lest unknowns
Engulf thee in the night!

· 265 ·

I felt my life with both my hands
To see if it was there;
I held my spirit to the glass
To prove it possibler;

I turned my being round and round
And paused at every pound
To ask the owner's name for doubt
That I should know the sound;

I judged my features, jarred my hair,
I pushed my dimples by
And waited—if they twinkled back
Conviction might, of me.

I told myself, "Take courage, friend,
That was a former time—
But we might learn to like the heaven
As well as our old home!"

· 266 ·

The drop that wrestles in the sea
Forgets her own locality
  As I in thee.

She knows herself an offering small,
Yet small, she sighs, if all is all
  How larger be?

The ocean smiles at her conceit
But she, forgetting Amphitrite,
  Pleads "Me?"

· 267 ·

We talked with each other about each other
Though neither of us spoke—
We were listening to the seconds' races
And the hoofs of the clock.

Pausing in front of our palsied faces,
Time compassion took;
Arks of reprieve he offered to us,
Ararats we took.

· 268 ·

ME, CHANGE! Me, alter! Then I will
When on the everlasting hill
A smaller purple grows
At sunset, or a lesser glow
Flickers upon Cordillera
At day's superior close!

· 269 ·

FALSEHOOD of thee could I suppose,
'Twould undermine the sill
To which my faith pinned block by block
Her cedar citadel.

· 270 ·

A TONGUE to tell him I am true!
Its fee to be of gold.
Had nature in her monstrous house
A single ragged child

To earn a mine would run
That interdicted way
And tell him—charge thee, speak it plain!—
That so far truth is true?

And answer what I do,
Beginning with the day
That night begun—nay, midnight 'twas—
Since midnight happened, say.

If once more—pardon, boy,
The magnitude—thou may
Enlarge my message, if too vast
Another lad help thee,

Thy pay in diamonds be,
And his in solid gold.
Say rubies if he hesitate,
My message must be told!

Say last I said was this:
That when the hills come down
And hold no higher than the plain
My bond have just begun;

And when the heavens disband
And Deity conclude,
Then look for me—be sure you say
Least figure on the road.

· 271 ·

My eye is fuller than my vase,
Her cargo is of dew,
And still my heart my eye outweighs
East India for you!

· 272 ·

Bind me, I still can sing.
Banish, my mandolin
Strikes true within.

Slay, and my soul shall rise
Chanting to paradise,
Still thine.

· 273 ·

'Twas here my summer paused,
What ripeness after then
To other scene or other soul?
My sentence had begun,

To winter to remove,
With winter to abide.
Go manacle your icicle
Against your tropic bride!

· 274 ·

Because the bee may blameless hum
For thee a bee do I become.
List even unto me!

Because the flowers unafraid
May lift a look on thine, a maid
Alway a flower would be.

Nor robins, robins need not hide
When thou upon their crypts intrude.
So wings bestow on me,

Or petals, or a dower of buzz,
That bee to ride, or flower of furze,
I that way worship thee.

· 275 ·

Rearrange a wife's affection?
When they dislocate my brain,
Amputate my freckled bosom,
Make me bearded like a man!

Blush, my spirit, in thy fastness,
Blush, my unacknowledged clay,
Seven years of troth have taught thee
More than wifehood ever may!

Love that never leaped its socket,
Trust entrenched in narrow pain,
Constancy through fire awarded,
Anguish bare of anodyne,

Burden borne so far triumphant
None suspect me of the crown,
For I wear the thorns till sunset,
Then my diadem put on.

Big my secret, but it's bandaged,
It will never get away
Till the day its weary keeper
Leads it through the grave to thee.

· 276 ·

THE world stands solemner to me
Since I was wed to him;
A modesty befits the soul
That bears another's name;

A doubt if it be fair indeed
To wear that perfect pearl
The man upon the woman binds
To clasp her soul for all;

A prayer that it more angel prove,
A whiter gift within,
To that munificence that chose
So unadorned a queen:

A gratitude that such be true—
It had esteemed the dream
Too beautiful for shape to prove
Or posture to redeem!

· 277 ·

I'VE none to tell me to but thee,
So when thou failest, nobody.
  It was a little tie,
It just held two, nor those it held,
Since somewhere thy sweet face has spilled
  Beyond my boundary.

If things were opposite, and me,
And me it were that ebbed from thee
  On some unanswering shore,
Wouldst thou seek so? Just say!
That I the answer may pursue
Unto the lips it eddied through,
  So—overtaking thee.

· 278 ·

ROBBED by death, but that was easy,
To the failing eye
I could hold the latest glowing;
Robbed by liberty

For her jugular defenses,
This, too, I endured,
Hint of glory it afforded
For the brave beloved.

Fraud of distance, fraud of danger,
Fraud of death to bear,
It is bounty, to suspense's
Vague calamity,

Staking our entire possession
On a hair's result,
Then seesawing coolly on it,
Trying if it split.

· 279 ·

HE FOUND my being, set it up,
Adjusted it to place,
Then carved his name upon it,
And bade it to the east

Be faithful in his absence
And he would come again
With equipage of amber,
That time, to take it home.

· 280 ·

I LEARNED at least what home could be,
How ignorant I had been
Of pretty ways of covenant,
How awkward at the hymn

Round our new fireside, but for this,
This pattern of the way,
Whose memory drowns me like the dip
Of a celestial sea.

What mornings in our garden, guessed,
What bees for us to hum,
With only birds to interrupt
The ripple of our theme.

And task for both when play be done,
Your problem of the brain,
And mine some foolisher effect,
A ruffle, or a tune.

The afternoons together spent,
And twilight in the lanes,
Some ministry to poorer lives
Seen poorest through our gains.

And then return, and night and home,
A new diviner care,
Till sunrise call us back to scene
Transmuted, vivider.

This seems a home and home is not,
But what that place could be
Afflicts me as a setting sun
Where dawn knows how to be!

· 281 ·

HE WAS my host, he was my guest,
I never to this day
If I invited him could tell
Or he invited me.

So infinite our interview,
So intimate indeed,
Analysis like capsule seemed
To keeper of the seed.

· 282 ·

BECAUSE that you are going
And never coming back
And I, however accurate,
May overlook your track,

Because that death is final,
However first it be,
This instant be suspended
Above mortality.

Significance that each has lived
The other to detect—
Discovery not God Himself
Could now annihilate.

Eternity, presumption,
The instant I perceive
That you, who were existence,
Yourself forgot to live.

The "life that is" will then have been
A thing I never knew,
As paradise fictitious
Until the realm of you.

The "life that is to be" to me
A residence too plain
Unless in my Redeemer's face
I recognize your own.

Of immortality who doubts
He may exchange with me,
Curtailed by your obscuring face
Of everything but he.

Of heaven and hell I also yield
The right to reprehend
To whoso would commute this face
For his less priceless friend.

If "God is love" as He admits,
We think that He must be
Because He is a jealous God
He tells us certainly.

If "all is possible" with Him
As He besides concedes,
He will refund us finally
Our confiscated gods.[17]

· 283 ·

SEVERER service of myself
I hastened to demand
To fill the awful vacuum
Your life had left behind.

I worried nature with my wheels
When hers had ceased to run;
When she had put away her work
My own had just begun.

I strove to weary brain and bone,
To harass, to fatigue
The glittering retinue of nerves,
Vitality to clog.

[17] This poem was published in *The Life and Mind of Emily Dickinson*, by Genevieve Taggard, 1930. Three copies in Emily's handwriting are not in all respects identical, but are not different enough to constitute three separate versions. The Taggard version was the one Emily sent to Colonel Higginson.

To some dull comfort those obtain
Who put a head away
They knew the hair to, and forget
The color of the day.

Affliction would not be appeased,
The darkness braced as firm
As all my stratagem had been
The midnight to confirm.

No drug for consciousness can be;
Alternative to die
Is nature's only pharmacy
For being's malady.

· 284 ·

A WORLD made penniless by his departure
Of minor systems begs,
But sustenance is of the spirit,
The stars but dregs.

· 285 ·

THE most pathetic thing I do
Is play I hear from you;
I make believe until my heart
Almost believes it too.

But when I break it with the news,
"You knew it was not true,"
I wish I had not broken it,
Goliah—so would you.

· 286 ·

To WAIT an hour is long
If love be just beyond;
To wait eternity is short
If love be at the end.

· 287 ·

To BE forgot by thee
Surpasses memory
Of other minds;
The heart cannot forget
Unless it contemplate
What it declines.

I was considered, then,
Raised from oblivion
A single time
To be remembered! What?
Worthy to be forgot
Is my renown!

For one must recollect
Before it can forget.

· 288 ·

MEETING by accident,
We hovered by design.
As often as a century
An error so divine

Is ratified by destiny;
But destiny is old
And economical of bliss
As Midas is of gold.

· 289 ·

We met as sparks—diverging flints
Sent various scattered ways;
We parted as the central flint
Were cloven with an adze,

Subsisting on the light we bore
Before we felt the dark,
A flint unto this day perhaps
But for that single spark.

· 290 ·

How sick to wait
In any place but thine
I knew last night
When someone tried to twine,

Thinking perhaps
That I looked tired or alone
Or breaking almost
With unspoken pain,

And I turned, ducal,
That right was thine!
One port suffices
For a brig like mine.

Ours be the tossing,
Wild though the sea,
Rather than a mooring
Unshared by thee.

Ours be the cargo
Unladen here
Rather than the Spicy Isles
And thou not there.

· 291 ·

WHEN I see not, I better see
Through faith. My hazel eye
Has periods of shutting, but
No lid has memory.

For often, all my sense obscured,
I equally behold,
As someone held a light unto
The features so beloved,

And I arise, and in my dream
Do thee distinguished grace,
Till jealous daylight interrupt
And mar thy perfectness.

· 292 ·

ONE year ago jots what?
God spell the word, I can't!
Was 't grace? Not that.
Was 't glory? That will do.
Spell slower! Glory, 'twas just you!

Such anniversary shall be
Sometimes, not often, in eternity,
When farther parted than the common woe,
Look, feed upon each other's faces so
In doubtful meal, if it be true
Their banquet 's real.

I tasted careless then.
I did not know the wine
Came once a world, did you?
Oh, had you told me so,
This thirst would blister easier now!

You said it hurt you most,
Mine was an acorn's breast
And could not know how fondness grew
In shaggier vest.

Perhaps I couldn't.
But had you looked in,
A giant eye to eye with you had been,
No acorn then!

So, twelve months ago
We breathed,
Then dropped the air.
Which bore it best?
Was this the patientest
Because it was a child, you know,
And could not value air?

If to be "elder" mean most pain,
I'm old enough today, I'm certain, then.
As old as thee? How soon?
One birthday more, or ten?
Let me choose! . . .
Ah! Sir, none!

· 293 ·

Sweet, you forgot, but I remembered
Every time for two,
So that the sum be never hindered
Through decay of you.

Say if I erred? Accuse my farthings,
Blame the little hand
Happy it be for you a beggar's,
Seeking more to spend.

Just to be rich, to waste my guineas
On so best a heart!
Just to be poor, for barefoot vision
You, sweet, shut me out![18]

· 294 ·

No matter now, sweet,
But when I'm earl
Won't you wish you'd spoken
To that dull girl?

Trivial a word just,
Trivial a smile,
But won't you wish you'd spared one
When I'm earl?

I shan't need it then,
Crests will do;
Eagles on my buckles,
On my belt, too;

Ermine my familiar gown—
Say, sweet, then
Won't you wish you'd smiled
Just me upon?

[18] A slightly different version of the final stanza was sent to Samuel Bowles:

Just to be rich, to waste my guinea
On so broad a heart!
Just to be poor, for barefoot pleasure
You, Sir, shut me out!

· 295 ·

He forgot and I remembered,
'Twas an everyday affair
Long ago as Christ and Peter
Warmed them at the temple fire.

"Thou wert with him?" quoth the damsel.
"No," said Peter, " 'twasn't me."
Jesus merely looked at Peter—
Could I do aught else to thee?

· 296 ·

What shall I do when the summer troubles?
What, when the rose is ripe?
What, when the eggs fly off in music
From the maple keep?

What shall I do when the skies a-chirrup
Drop a tune on me?
When the bee hangs all noon in the buttercup,
What will become of me?

Oh, when the squirrel fills his pockets
And the berries stare,
How can I bear their jocund faces
Thou from here so far?

'Twouldn't afflict a robin,
All his goods have wings,
I do not fly—so wherefore
My perennial things?

· 297 ·

'Twas love, not me,
Oh, punish, pray!
The real one died for thee,
Trust Him, not me.

Such guilt to love the most!
Doom it beyond the rest,
Forgive it last,
'Twas base as Jesus', 'most!

Let justice not mistake,
We two looked so alike,
Which was the guilty sake,
'Twas love's—now strike!

· 298 ·

Did we disobey him
Just one time?
Charged us to forget him,
But we couldn't learn.

Were himself such a dunce
What would we do?
Love the dull lad best—
Oh, wouldn't you?

· 299 ·

If blame be my side forfeit me,
But doom me not to forfeit thee.
To forfeit thee? The very name
Is exile from belief and home!

· 300 ·

THE court is far away,
No umpire have I;
My sov'reign is offended,
To gain his grace I'd die!

I'll seek his royal feet,
I'll say, "Remember, King,
Thou shalt thyself one day, a child,
Implore a larger thing.

"That empire is of czars
As small they say as I—
Grant me that day the royalty
To intercede for thee!"

· 301 ·

I'VE dropped my brain, my soul is numb,
The veins that used to run
Stop palsied, 'tis paralysis
Done perfecter in stone.

Vitality is carved and cool,
My nerve in marble lies,
A breathing woman yesterday
Endowed with paradise.

Not dumb, I had a sort that moved,
A sense that smote and stirred,
Instincts for dance, a caper part,
An aptitude for bird.

Who wrought Carrara in me
And chiseled all my tune,
Were it a witchcraft, were it death,
I've still a chance to strain

To being, somewhere—motion, breath—
Though centuries beyond,
And every limit a decade
I'll shiver, satisfied.

· 302 ·

I'LL tell thee all—how blank it grew,
How midnight felt at first to me,
How all the clocks stopped in the world,
And sunshine pinched me, 'twas so cold.

Then how the grief got sleepy some,
As if my soul were deaf and dumb,
Just making signs across to thee
That this way thou couldst speak to me.

I'll tell you how I tried to keep
A smile to show you when, this deep
All waded, we look back for play
At those old times in Calvary.

Forgive me, if the grave seem slow
For eagerness to look at thee!
Forgive me, if to touch thy frost
Outvisions paradise!

· 303 ·

WERT thou but ill that I might show thee
How long a day I could endure
Though thine attention stop not on me,
Nor the least signal mine assure;

Wert thou but stranger in ungracious country
And mine the door
Thou paused at for a doubtful bounty,
Thou'd pause no more.

Accused wert thou, and myself tribunal,
Convicted, sentenced, ermine not to me
Half the distinction thy reverse to follow,
Just to partake the infamy.

The tenant of the narrow cottage wert thou,
Permit to be
The housewife in thy low attendance
Contenteth me.

No service hast thou I would not achieve it,
To die or live,
The first, sweet, proved I ere I saw thee,
For life means love!

· 304 ·

If I'm lost now, that I was found
Shall still my transport be—
That once on me those jasper gates
Blazed open suddenly;

That in my awkward gazing face
The angels softly peered
And touched me with their fleeces
Almost as if they cared.

I'm banished now—you know it!
How foreign that can be
You'll know, Sir, when the Savior's face
Turns so, away from you!

· 305 ·

Too scanty 'twas to die for you,
The merest Greek could that;
The living, sweet, is costlier—
I offer even that.

The dying is a trifle, past,
But living—this include
The dying multifold without
The respite to be dead.

· 306 ·

This chasm, sweet, upon my life,
I mention it to you;
When sunrise through a fissure drop
The day must follow too.

If we demur, its gaping sides
Disclose as 'twere a tomb
Ourself am lying straight wherein,
The favorite of doom.

When it has just contained a life
Then, darling, it will close,
And yet, so bolder every day,
So turbulent it grows,

I'm tempted half to stitch it up
With a remaining breath
I should not miss in yielding, though
To him it would be death.

And so I bear it big about
My burial before—
A life quite ready to depart
Can harass me no more.

· 307 ·

'TWAS my one glory—
Let it be
Remembered
I was owned of thee.

· 308 ·

NOR mountain hinder me,
Nor sea—
Who's Baltic?
Who's Cordillera?[19]

· 309 ·

SIFT her from brow to bare foot,
Strain, till your last surmise
Drop like a tapestry away
Before the fire's eyes;

Winnow her finest fondness,
But hallow just the snow
Intact in everlasting flake
Oh, cavalier, for you!

· 310 ·

THE voice that stands for floods to me
Is sterile borne to some;
The face that makes the morning mean
Glows impotent on them.

[19] Though written on the same page of manuscript, Emily drew a line between 307 and 308, indicating that they are separate poems.

What difference in substance lies,
That what is sum to me
By other financiers be deemed
Exclusive poverty!

· 311 ·

'Twould ease a butterfly,
Elate a bee.
Thou'rt neither,
Neither thy capacity.

But blossom were I,
I would rather be
Thy moment
Than a bee's eternity.

Content of fading
Is enough for me,
Fade I unto divinity,

And dying, lifetime,
Ample as the eye
Her least attention raise on me.

· 312 ·

Still own thee—still thou art
What surgeons call alive,
Though slipping, slipping I perceive
To thy reportless grave.

Which question shall I clutch?
What answer wrest from thee
Before thou dost exude away
In the recall-less sea?

· 313 ·

On the world you colored
Morning painted rose,
Idle his vermilion,
Aimless crept the glows

Over realms of orchards
I the day before
Conquered with the robin.
Misery, how fair

Till your wrinkled finger
Pushed the sun away,
Midnight's awful pattern
In the goods of day.

· 314 ·

My heart ran so to thee
It would not wait for me,
And I discouraged grew
And drew away,

For whatsoe'er my pace
He first achieve thy face,
How general a grace
Allotted two!

Not in malignity
Mentioned I this to thee,
Had he obliquity
Soonest to share,

But for the greed of him
Boasting my premium,
Basking in Bethlehem
Ere I be there.

· 315 ·

LIVES he in any other world
My faith cannot reply;
Before it was imperative
All was distinct to me.

· 316 ·

TRIED always and condemned by thee,
Permit me this reprieve,
That trying, I may earn the look
For which I cease to live.[20]

· 317 ·

IT CAME his turn to beg.
The begging for the life
Is different from another alms,
'Tis penury in chief.

I scanned his narrow realm,
I gave him leave to live
Lest gratitude revive the snake,
Though smuggled his reprieve.

· 318 ·

THE pile of years is not so high
As when you came before,
But it is rising every day
From recollection's floor,

[20] The two quatrains 315 and 316, though written on a single scrap of paper, appear to be separate poems.

And while by standing on my heart
I still can reach the top,
Efface the mountain with your face
And catch me ere I drop!

· 319 ·

THE thrill came slowly like a boon
For centuries delayed,
Its fitness growing like the flood
In sumptuous solitude.

The desolation only missed
While rapture changed its dress
And stood amazed before the change
In ravished holiness.

· 320 ·

I GROPED for him before I knew
With solemn nameless need,
All other bounty sudden chaff
For this foreshadowed food

Which others taste and spurn and slight,
Though I within suppose
That consecrated it could be
The only food that grows.

· 321 ·

YOU said that I was "great" one day,
Then "great" it be, if that please thee,
Or "small," or any size at all—
Nay, I'm the size suit thee.

Tall, like the stag, would that?
Or cower, like the wren?
Or other heights of other ones
I've seen?

Tell which, it's dull to guess,
And I must be
Rhinoceros or mouse at once
For thee.

So say if Queen it be
Or page,
Please thee I'm that
Or naught,

Or other thing,
If other thing there be,
With just this—
I suit thee.

· 322 ·

EXTOL thee—could I—then I will
By saying nothing new,
But just the tritest truth
That thou art heavenly.

Perceiving thee is evidence
That we are of the sky;
Partaking thee, a guaranty
Of immortality.

· 323 ·

Through what transports of patience
I reached the stolid bliss
To breathe my blank without thee,
Attest me this and this.

By that bleak exultation
I won as near as this
Thy privilege of dying—
Abbreviate me this.

· 324 ·

Mute thy coronation,
Meek my "Vive le roi!"
Fold a tiny courtier
In thine ermine, Sir,

There to rest revering
Till, the pageant by,
I can murmur, broken,
"Master, it was I!"

· 325 ·

The smouldering embers blush.
Oh, heart within the coal,
Hast thou survived so many years?
The smouldering embers smile.

Soft stirs the news of light,
The stolid seconds glow,
One requisite has fire that lasts
Prometheus never knew.

· 326 ·

LONG years apart can make no breach
A second cannot fill;
The absence of the witch does not
Invalidate the spell.

The embers of a thousand years,
Uncovered by the hand
That fondled them when they were fire,
Will gleam and understand.

· 327 ·

OF WHOM so dear
The name to hear
Illumines with a glow

As intimate,
As fugitive,
As sunset on the snow.

· 328 ·

TO DIE without the dying
And live without the life—
This is the hardest miracle
Propounded to belief.

· 329 ·

TO BREAK so vast a heart
Required a blow as vast;
No zephyr felled this cedar straight,
'Twas undeservéd blast.

· 330 ·

IT CAME at last, but prompter death
Had occupied the house,
His pallid furniture arranged
And his metallic peace.

Oh, faithful frost that kept the date!
Had love as punctual been,
Delight had aggrandized the gate
And blocked the coming in.

· 331 ·

YOU constituted time.
I deemed eternity
A revelation of yourself.
'Twas therefore Deity.

The Absolute removed
The relative away,
That I unto Himself adjust
My slow idolatry.

· 332 ·

SOMEWHERE upon the general earth
Itself exist today—
The magic, passive but extant,
That consecrated me.

Indifferent seasons doubtless play
Where I, for right to be,
Would pawn each atom that I am
But immortality,

Reserving that but just to prove
Another date of thee.
Oh, God of width, do not for us
Curtail eternity!

· 333 ·

The face I carry with me last,
When I go out of time,
To take my rank by, in the west,
That face will just be thine.

I'll hand it to the angel,
"That, Sir, was my degree
In kingdoms you have heard the raised
Refer to possibly."

He'll take it, scan it, step aside,
Return with such a crown
As Gabriel never capered at,
And beg me put it on.

And then he'll turn me round and round
To an admiring sky,
As one that bore her master's name—
Sufficient royalty!

· 334 ·

When one has given up one's life
The parting with the rest
Feels easy, as when day lets go
Entirely the west;

The peaks that lingered last
Remain in her regret
As scarcely as the iodine
Upon the cataract.

· 335 ·

Recollect the face of me
When in thy felicity,
Due in paradise today,
Guest of mine assuredly,

Other courtesies have been,
Other courtesy may be.
We commend ourselves to thee,
Paragon of chivalry.

· 336 ·

While it is alive, until death touches it,
While it and I lap one air,
Dwell in one blood under one sacrament,
Show me division can split or pare!

Love is like life, merely longer;
Love is like death, daring the grave;
Love is the fellow of the resurrection
Scooping up the dust and chanting "Live!"

· 337 ·

So GIVE me back to death,
The death I never feared
Except that it deprived of thee;
And now, by life deprived,
In my own grave I breathe
And estimate its size—
Its size is all that hell can guess
And all that heaven surmise.

The White Exploit

· 338 ·

THOSE who have been in the grave the longest,
Those who begin today,
Equally perish from our practice.
Death is the further way.

Foot of the bold did least attempt it,
It is the white exploit
Once to achieve annuls the power
Once to communicate.

THE FINAL INCH

· 339 ·

'TWAS like a maelstrom, with a notch
That nearer every day
Kept narrowing its boiling wheel
Until the agony

Toyed coolly with the final inch
Of your delirious hem,
And you dropped, lost, when something broke
And let you from a dream

As if a goblin with a gauge
Kept measuring the hours,
Until you felt your second weigh
Helpless in his paws,

And not a sinew, stirred, could help,
And sense was setting numb,
When God remembered, and the fiend
Let go then, overcome;

As if your sentence stood pronounced,
And you were frozen led
From dungeon's luxury of doubt
To gibbets and the dead;

And when the film had stitched your eyes,
A creature gasped "Reprieve!"
Which anguish was the utterest then,
To perish, or to live?

· 340 ·

THE manner of its death,
When certain it must die,
'Tis deemed a privilege to choose,
'Twas Major André's way.

When choice of life is past,
There yet remains a love
Its little fate to stipulate.
How small in those who live

The miracle to tease
With babble of the styles—
How "they are dying mostly, now,"
And customs at "St. James'!"

· 341 ·

WATER makes many beds
For those averse to sleep,
Its awful chamber open stands,
Its curtains blandly sweep;

Abhorrent is the rest
In undulating rooms
Whose amplitude no clock invades,
Whose morning never comes.

· 342 ·

THE waters chased him as he fled,
Not daring look behind;
A billow whispered in his ear,
"Come home with me, my friend!

My parlor is of shriven glass,
My pantry has a fish
For every palate in the year."
To this revolting bliss
The object floating at his side
Made no distinct reply.

· 343 ·

EACH second is the last,
Perhaps, recalls the man
Just measuring unconsciousness
The sea and spar between.

To fail within a chance
How terribler a thing
Than perish from the chance's list
Before the perishing!

· 344 ·

How the waters closed above him
We shall never know;
How he stretched his anguish to us,
That is covered too.

Spreads the pond her base of lilies
Bold above the boy
Whose unclaiméd hat and jacket
Sum the history.

· 345 ·

FORTITUDE incarnate
Here is laid away
In the swift partitions
Of the awful sea.

Babble of the happy,
Cavil of the bold,
Hoary the fruition,
But the sea is old.

Edifice of ocean,
Thy tumultuous rooms
Suit me at a venture
Better than the tombs.

· 346 ·

HE SCANNED it, staggered, dropped the loop
To past or period,
Caught helpless at a sense as if
His mind were going blind;

Groped up to see if God was there,
Groped backward at himself,
Caressed a trigger absently
And wandered out of life.

· 347 ·

A DYING tiger moaned for drink;
I hunted all the sand,
I caught the dripping of a rock
And bore it in my hand;

His mighty balls in death were thick,
But searching I could see
A vision on the retina
Of water and of me.

'Twas not my blame who sped too slow,
'Twas not his blame who died
While I was reaching him, but 'twas
The fact that he was dead.

· 348 ·

In crashing timbers buried
There breathed a man;
Outside the spades were plying,
The lungs within.

Could he know they sought him!
Could they know he breathed!
Horrid sand partition,
Neither could be heard.

Never slacked the diggers,
But when spades had done,
Oh, recompense of anguish,
He was dying then.

Many things are fruitless,
'Tis a baffling earth;
But there is no gratitude
Like the grace of death.

· 349 ·

The harm of years is on him,
The infamy of time.
Depose him like a fashion
And give dominion room!

Forget his morning forces,
The glory of decay
Is a denuded pageant
Beside vitality.

· 350 ·

Two travelers perishing in snow.
The forests as they froze
Together heard them strengthening
Each other with the news

That heaven, if heaven, must contain
What either left behind;
And then the cheer too solemn grew
For language, and the wind

Long steps across the features took
That love had touched that morn
With reverential hyacinth.
The taleless days went on

Till mystery impatient drew,
And those they left behind
Led absent, were procured of heaven
As those first furnished said.

· 351 ·

PAIN has but one acquaintance
And that is death;
Each one unto the other
Society enough.

Pain is the junior party
By just a second's right;
Death tenderly assists him
And then absconds from sight.

· 352 ·

'TWAS crisis. All the length had passed,
That dull benumbing time
There is in fever or event,
And now the chance had come,

The instant holding in its claw
The privilege to live,
Or warrant to report the soul
The other side the grave.

The muscles grappled as with leads
That would not let the will;
The spirit shook the adamant
But could not make it feel.

The second poised—debated—shot—
Another had begun.
And simultaneously a soul
Escaped the house unseen.

· 353 ·

CRISIS is a hair
Toward which forces creep,
Past which forces retrograde.
If it come in sleep,

To suspend the breath
Is the most we can,
Ignorant is it life or death
Nicely balancing.

Let an instant push,
Or an atom press,
Or a circle hesitate
In circumference,

It may jolt the hand
That adjusts the hair
That secures eternity
From presenting here.

· 354 ·

SAID death to passion, "Give of thine
An acre unto me."
Said passion, through contracting breaths,
"A thousand times thee nay!"

Bore death from passion all his east;
He, sov'reign as the sun,
Resituated in the west,
And the debate was done.

· 355 ·

DEATH-WARRANTS are supposed to be
An enginery of equity—
  A merciful mistake.
A pencil in an idol's hand
A devotee has oft consigned
  To crucifix or block.

· 356 ·

THIS that would greet an hour ago
Is quaintest distance now.
Had it a guest from paradise
Nor glow would it, nor bow;

Had it a summons from the noon
Nor beam would it, nor warm—
Match me the silver reticence!
Match me the solid calm!

· 357 ·

THE vastest earthly day
Is shrunken small
By one defaulting face
Behind a pall.

· 358 ·

OH, GIVE it motion—deck it sweet
With artery and vein!
Upon its fastened lips lay words.
Affiance it again

To that pink stranger we call dust,
Acquainted more with that
Than with this horizontal one
That will not lift its hat.

· 359 ·

COULD live—*did* live. Could die—*did* die.
Could smile upon the whole
Through faith in one he met not
To introduce his soul.

Could go from scene familiar
To an untraversed spot;
Could contemplate the journey
With unpuzzled heart.

Such trust had one among us,
Among us *not* today.
We who saw the launching
Never sailed the bay!

· 360 ·

DYING! To be afraid of thee
One must to thine artillery
  Have left exposed a friend.
Than thine old arrow is a shot
Delivered straighter to the heart,
  The leaving love behind.

Not for itself the dust is shy,
But, enemy, belovéd be
  Thy batteries' divorce.
Fight sternly in a dying eye
Two armies, love and certainty,
  And love and the reverse.

· 361 ·

Frigid and sweet her parting face,
Frigid and fleet my feet,
Alien and vain whatever clime,
Acrid whatever fate;

Given to me without the suit
Riches and name and realm—
Who was she, to withhold from me
Hemisphere and home?

· 362 ·

We miss her, not because we see.
The absence of an eye,
Except its mind accompany,
Impair society

As slightly as the routes of stars,
Ourselves asleep below;
We know that their superior eyes
Include us as they go.

· 363 ·

This docile one inter,
While we who dare to live
Arraign the sunny brevity
That sparkles in the grave.

Of her departing span
No wilderness retain,
As dauntless in the house of death
As if it were her own

· 364 ·

So HAS a daisy vanished
From the fields today,
So tiptoed many a slipper
To paradise away,

Oozed so in crimson bubbles
Day's departing tide,
Blooming, tripping, flowing—
Are ye then with God?

· 365 ·

WHATEVER it is she has tried it,
Awful Father of love.
Is not ours the chastising?
Do not chastise the dove!

Not for ourselves, petition,
Nothing is left to pray,
When a subject is finished
Words are withered away.

Only lest she be lonely
In Thy beautiful house,
Give her for her transgression
License to think of us.

· 366 ·

ON THAT dear frame the years had worn,
Yet precious as the house
In which we first experienced light
The witnessing, to us.

Precious! It was conceiveless fair,
As hands the grave had grimed
Should softly place within our own,
Denying that they died.

· 367 ·

As SLEIGH bells seem in summer
Or bees at Christmas show,
So foreign, so fictitious,
The individuals do

Repealed from observation—
A party whom we knew
More distant in an instant
Than dawn in Timbuctoo.

· 368 ·

ENDOW the living with the tears
You squander on the dead
And they were men and women now
Around your fireside,

Instead of passive creatures
Denied the cherishing
Till they the cherishing deny
With death's ethereal scorn.

· 369 ·

WHICH misses most, the hand that tends,
Or heart so gently borne
'Tis twice as heavy as it was
Because the hand is gone?

Which blesses most, the lip that can,
Or that that went to sleep
With "if I could" endeavoring,
Without the strength to shape?

· 370 ·

DEATH leaves us homesick who behind,
Except that it is gone,
Are ignorant of its concern
As if it were not born.

Through all its former places we
Like individuals go
Who something lost, the seeking for
Is all that's left them now.

· 371 ·

DEATH is potential to that man
Who dies, and to his friend;
Beyond that, unconspicuous
To anyone but God.

Of these two, God remembers
The longest, for the friend
Is subsequent, and therefore
Itself dissolved of God.

· 372 ·

"WAS not" was all the statement.
The unpretension stuns,
Perhaps the comprehension;
They wore no lexicons.

But lest our speculation
In inanition die,
Because "God took him," mention—
That was philology.[21]

· 373 ·

Two were immortal twice,
The privilege of few.
Eternity in time obtained,
Reversed divinity,

That our ignoble eyes
The quality perceive
Of paradise superlative
Through their comparative.

· 374 ·

DEATH is the supple suitor
That wins at last.
It is a stealthy wooing,
Conducted first

By pallid innuendoes
And dim approach,
But brave at last with bugles
And a bisected coach

It bears away in triumph
To troth unknown
And kindred as responsive
As porcelain.

[21] Genesis V:24.

· 375 ·

WITH pinions of disdain
The soul can farther fly
Than any feather certified
By ornithology.

It wafts this sordid flesh
Beyond its slow control,
And during its electric spell
The body is a soul.

Instructing by itself,
How little work it be
To put off filaments like this
For immortality!

· 376 ·

IT KNEW no lapse nor diminution,
But large, serene,
Glowed on until through dissolution
It failed from men.

I could not deem these planetary forces
Annulled,
But suffered an exchange of territory
Or world.

· 377 ·

HE LIVED the life of ambush
And went the way of dusk,
And now against his subtle name
There stands an asterisk

As confident of him as we—
Impregnable we are—
The whole of immortality
Intrenched within a star.

· 378 ·

GATHERED into the earth
And out of story,
Gathered to that strange fame,
That lonesome glory
That hath no omen here
But awe.

· 379 ·

'TIS not that dying hurts us so,
'Tis living hurts us more.
But dying is a different way,
A kind behind the door,

The southern custom of the birds
That ere the frosts are due
Accepts a better latitude.
We are the birds that stay—

The shiverers 'round farmers' doors,
For whose reluctant crumb
We stipulate, till pitying snows
Persuade our feathers home.

· 380 ·

As plan for noon and plan for night,
So differ life and death
In positive prospective.
The foot upon the earth

At distance and achievement strains;
The foot upon the grave
Makes effort at conclusion,
Assisted faint of love.

· 381 ·

The opening and the close
Of being are alike,
Or differ, if they do,
As bloom upon a stalk

That from an equal seed
Unto an equal bud
Go parallel, perfected
In that they have decayed.

· 382 ·

Left in immortal youth
On that low plain
That hath nor peradventure
Nor again;

Ransomed from years,
Sequestered from decay,
Canceled like dawn
In comprehensive day!

· 383 ·

SWEET safe houses—glad gay houses—
Sealed so stately tight!
Lids of steel on lids of marble
Locking bare feet out.

Brooks of plush in banks of satin
Not so softly fall
As the laughter and the whisper
From their people pearl.

No bald death affront their parlors,
No bold sickness come
To deface their stately treasures.
Anguish and the tomb

Hum by, in muffled coaches,
Lest they wonder why
Any, for the press of smiling,
Interrupt to die.

· 384 ·

BACK from the cordial grave I drag thee,
He shall not take thy hand
Nor put his spacious arm around thee—
That none can understand.

· 385 ·

MORE than the grave is closed to me—
The grave and that eternity
  To which the grave adheres.
I cling to nowhere till I fall.
The crash of nothing, yet of all,
  How similar appears!

· 386 ·

A COFFIN is a small domain
Yet able to contain
A rudiment of paradise
In its diminished plane.

A grave is a restricted breadth
Yet ampler than the sun
And all the seas he populates
And lands he looks upon,

To him who on its low repose
Bestows a single friend—
Circumference without relief,
Or estimate, or end.

· 387 ·

LAIN in nature, so suffice us
The enchantless pod
When we advertise existence
For the missing seed.

Maddest heart that God created
Cannot move a sod
Pasted by the simple summer
On the soldered dead.

· 388 ·

Snow beneath whose chilly softness
Some that never lay
Make their first repose this winter,
I admonish thee

Blanket wealthier the neighbor
We so new bestow
Than thine acclimated creature—
Wilt thou, Russian snow?

· 389 ·

Who occupies this house?
A stranger I must judge
Since no one knows his circumstance.
'Tis well the name and age

Are writ upon the door
Or I should fear to pause
Where not so much as honest dog
Approach encourages.

It seems a curious town,
Some houses very old,
Some newly raised this afternoon.
Were I compelled to build

It should not be among
Inhabitants so still,
But where the birds assemble
And boys were possible.

Before myself was born
'Twas settled, so they say,
A territory for the ghosts
And squirrels formerly,

Until a pioneer,
As settlers often do,
Liking the quiet of the place
Attracted more unto;

And from a settlement
A capital has grown,
Distinguished for the gravity
Of every citizen.

The owner of this house
A stranger he must be.
Eternity's acquaintances
Are mostly so to me.

· 390 ·

Knock with tremor; these are Caesars.
Should they be at home,
Flee as if you trod unthinking
On the foot of doom.

These seceded from your substance
Centuries ago;
Should they rend you with "How are you?"
What have you to show?

· 391 ·

How fortunate the grave,
All prizes to obtain,
Successful certain, if at last,
First suitor not in vain.

· 392 ·

Do PEOPLE moulder equally
They bury in the grave?
I do believe a species
As positively live

As I, who testify it,
Deny that I am dead
And fill my lungs for witness
From tanks above my head.

"I say to you," said Jesus,
"That there be standing here
A sort that shall not taste of death."
If Jesus was sincere

I need no further argue.
The statement of the Lord
Is not a controvertible.
He told me death was dead.

· 393 ·

UNDER the light, yet under,
Under the grass and the dirt,
Under the beetle's cellar,
Under the clover's foot,

Further than arm could stretch
Were it giant long,
Further than sunshine could
Were the day year long;

Over the light, yet over,
Over the arc of the bird,
Over the comet's chimney,
Over the cubit's head,

Further than guess can gallop,
Further than riddle ride—
Oh, for a disk to the distance
Between ourselves and the dead!

· 394 ·

There is a finished feeling
Experienced at graves—
A leisure of the future,
A wilderness of size,

By death's bold exhibition
Preciser what we are
And the eternal function
Enabled to infer.

· 395 ·

UPON concluded lives
There's nothing cooler falls
Than life's sweet calculations.
The mixing bells and palls

Makes lacerating tune
To ears the dying side;
'Tis coronal and funeral
Saluting in the road.

· 396 ·

THE chemical conviction
That naught be lost
Enable in disaster
My fractured trust.

The faces of the atoms
If I shall see,
How more the finished creatures
Departed me!

· 397 ·

A SHADE upon the mind there passes,
As when on noon
A cloud the mighty sun encloses,
Remembering

That some there be too numb to notice.
Oh, God!
Why give if Thou must take away
The loved?

· 398 ·

WITHIN thy grave! Oh, no,
But on some other flight!
Thou only camest to mankind
To rend it with "Good night!"

· 399 ·

"I WANT," it pleaded all its life.
"I want" was chief it said
When skill entreated it, the last,
And when so newly dead

I could not deem it late to hear
That single, steadfast sigh
The lips had placed, as with a "Please,"
Toward eternity.

· 400 ·

"GOOD night," because we must!
How intricate the dust!
I would *go* to know—
Oh, incognito!

Saucy, saucy seraph
To elude me so!
Father! They won't tell me!
Won't you tell them to?

· 401 ·

WHETHER they have forgotten,
Or are forgetting now,
Or never remembered,
Safer not to know.

Miseries of conjecture
Are a softer woe
Than a fact of iron
Hardened with "I know."

· 402 ·

WHAT did they do since I saw them?
Were they industrious?
So many questions to put them
Have I the eagerness

That could I snatch their faces,
That could their lips reply,
Not till the last was answered
Should they start for the sky!

Not if their party were waiting,
Not if to talk with me
Were to them now homesickness
After eternity;

Not if the just suspect me
And offer a reward
Would I restore my booty
To that bold person God![22]

[22] Written on a separate slip of paper pinned over the third stanza by Emily herself, the fourth stanza may have been intended as an alternative.

· 403 ·

THESE tested our horizon,
Then disappeared,
As birds before achieving
A latitude.

Our retrospection of them
A fixed delight,
But our anticipation
A dice—a doubt.

· 404 ·

SHE rose as high as his occasion
Then sought the dust,
And lower lay in low Westminster
For her brief crest.

· 405 ·

THE road to paradise is plain
And holds scarce one;
Not that it has not room,
But we presume
A dappled road
Is more preferred.
The guests of paradise are few,
Not me, nor you,
But unsuspected things;
Mines have no wings.

· 406 ·

THAT odd old man is dead a year,
We miss his stated hat;
'Twas such an evening bright and stiff
His faded lamp went out.

Who miss his antiquated wick?
Are any hoar for him?
Waits any indurated mate
His wrinkled coming home?

Oh, life, begun in fluent blood
And consummated dull!
Achievement contemplating this
Feels transitive and cool.

· 407 ·

THAT this should feel the need of death
The same as those that lived,
Is such a feat of irony
As never was achieved.

Not satisfied to ape the great
In his simplicity,
The small must die the same as he—
Oh, the audacity!

· 408 ·

PRAISE it—'tis dead, it cannot glow—
Warm this inclement ear
With the encomium it earned
Since it was gathered here.

Invest this alabaster zest
In the delights of dust
Remitted, since it flitted it,
In recusance august.

· 409 ·

'TIS anguish grander than delight,
'Tis resurrection pain—
The meeting bands of smitten face
We questioned to, again.

'Tis transport wild as thrills the graves
When cerements let go
And creatures clad in miracle
Go up by two and two.[23]

· 410 ·

How firm eternity must look
To crumbling men like me,
The only adamant estate
In all identity!

How mighty to the insecure
Thy physiognomy,
To whom not any face cohere
Unless concealed in thee!

[23] A variant of the last three lines appeared in the quatrain, "I'm thinking of that other morn," in *The Single Hound,* p. 96.

· 411 ·

As WATCHERS hang upon the east,
As beggars revel at a feast
By savory fancy spread,
As brooks in deserts babble sweet
On ear too far for the delight,
Heaven beguiles the tired.

As that same watcher, when the east
Opens the lid of amethyst
And lets the morning go,
That beggar, when an honored guest,
Those thirsty lips to flagons pressed,
Heaven to us, if true.

· 412 ·

THE fact that earth is heaven,
Whether heaven is heaven or not,
If not an affidavit
Of that specific spot,

Not only must confirm us
That it is not for us,
But that it would affront us
To dwell in such a place.

· 413 ·

THE hallowing of pain,
Like hallowing of heaven,
Obtains at a corporeal cost.
The summit is not given

To him who strives severe
At bottom of the hill,
But he who has achieved the top—
All is the price of all.

· 414 ·

"Houses," so the wise men tell me,
"Mansions"! Mansions must be warm,
Mansions cannot let the tears in,
Mansions must exclude the storm.

"Many mansions" by "His Father"—
I don't know him—snugly built.
Could the children find the way there
Some would even trudge tonight!

· 415 ·

How far is it to heaven?
As far as death this way.
Of fathom or of league beyond
Was no discovery.

How far is it to hell?
As far as death this way.
How far left hand the sepulchre
Defies topography.

· 416 ·

They leave us with the Infinite.
But He is not a man,
His fingers are the size of fists,
His fists, the size of men.

And whom He foundeth with His arm
As Himmaleh shall stand,
Gibraltar's everlasting shoe
Poised lightly on his hand.

So trust Him, comrade! You for you,
And I, for you and me.
Eternity is ample,
And quick enough, if true.

· 417 ·

THERE is a zone whose even years
No solstice interrupt,
Whose sun constructs perpetual noon,
Whose perfect seasons wait;

Whose summer set in summer till
The centuries of June
And centuries of August fuse
And consciousness is noon.

· 418 ·

SOME we see no more, tenements of wonder
Occupy, to us, though perhaps to them
Simpler are the days than the supposition
Their removing manners leave us to presume.

That oblique belief which we call conjecture
Grapples with a theme stubborn as sublime,
Able as the dust to equip its feature,
Adequate as drums to enlist the tomb.

· 419 ·

Not so the infinite relations.
Below
Division is adhesion's forfeit.
On high
Affliction but a speculation,
And woe
A fallacy, a figment
We knew.

· 420 ·

This dust and its feature,
Accredited today,
Will in a second future
Cease to identify.

This mind and its measure
A too minute area
For its enlarged inspection's
Comparison appear.

This world and its species
A too concluded show
For its absorbed attention's
Remotest scrutiny.

· 421 ·

You love the Lord you cannot see,
You write Him every day
A little note when you awake,
And further in the day

An ample letter—how you miss
And would delight to see—
But then, His house is but a step,
And mine's in heaven, you see.

· 422 ·

Of death I try to think like this:
The well in which they lay us
Is but the likeness of the brook
That menaced, not to slay us,
But to invite by that dismay
Which is the zest of sweetness
To the same flower Hesperian,
Decoying but to greet us.

I do remember when a child
With bolder playmates straying
To where a brook that seemed a sea
Withheld us by its roaring
From just a purple flower beyond
Until, constrained to clutch it,
Were doom itself the penalty,
The bravest leaped and clutched it.

· 423 ·

Aurora is the effort
Of the celestial face
Unconsciousness of perfectness
To simulate, to us.

· 424 ·

Of paradise' existence
All we know
Is the uncertain certainty,
But its vicinity infer
By its bisecting
Messenger.

· 425 ·

Taking up the fair ideal
Just to cast her down
When a fracture we discover,
Or a splintered crown,

Makes the heavens portable
And the gods a lie.
Doubtless Adam scowled at Eden
For *his* perjury!

Cherishing our poor ideal
Till in purer dress
We behold her glorified,
Comforts search like this,

Till the broken creatures
We adored for whole,
Stains all washed, transfigured, mended,
Meet us with a smile.

· 426 ·

Oh, future! Thou secreted peace
Or subterranean woe,
Is there no wandering route of grace
That leads away from thee—

No circuit sage of all the course
Descried by cunning men,
To balk thee of the innocence
Advancing to thy den?

· 427 ·

Besides this May we know
There is another.
How fair our speculations
  Of the foreigner!

Some know him whom we knew.
Sweet wonder, a nature be
Where saints and our plain-going neighbor
  Keep May!

· 428 ·

Image of light, adieu.
Thanks for the interview
  So long—so short.
Preceptor of the whole,
Coeval Cardinal,
  Impart, depart.

· 429 ·

There is a morn by men unseen,
Whose maids upon remoter green
Keep their seraphic May,
And all day long, with dance and game
And gambol I may never name,
Employ their holiday.

Here to light measure move the feet
Which walk no more the village street
Nor by the wood are found;
Here are the birds that sought the sun
When last year's distaff idle hung
And summer's brows were bound.

Ne'er saw I such a wondrous scene,
Ne'er such a ring on such a green,
Nor so serene array—
As if the stars some summer night
Should swing their cups of chrysolite
And revel till the day.

Like thee to dance, like thee to sing,
People upon that mystic green,
I ask each new May morn.
I wait thy far, fantastic bells
Announcing me in other dells
Unto the different dawn!

· 430 ·

If my bark sink
'Tis to another sea.[24]
Mortality's ground floor
Is immortality.

· 431 ·

The Infinite a sudden guest
Has been assumed to be,
But how can that stupendous come
Which never went away?

[24] "If my bark sinks, 'tis to another sea," is the final line of "A Poet's Hope," by William Ellery Channing.

Vital Light

· 432 ·

THE poets light but lamps,
Themselves go out;
The wicks they stimulate,
If vital light

Inhere as do the suns,
Each age a lens
Disseminating their
Circumference.

· 433 ·

THE mind lives on the heart
Like any parasite;
If that be full of meat
The mind is fat.

But if the heart be lean,
The stoutest mind will pine;
Throw not to the divine
Like dog a bone.[25]

[25] This poem is given as it appears in Emily's latest handwriting. An earlier version, of which there are three copies in writing of approximately the same date, was published in *The New England Quarterly*, April, 1932, with a different second stanza:

But if the heart omit,
Emaciate the wit.
The aliment of it
So absolute.

· 434 ·

SUCH are the inlets of the mind;
His outlets would you see,
Ascend with me the table-land
Of immortality.

· 435 ·

YOUR thoughts don't have words every day,
They come a single time
Like signal esoteric sips
Of sacramental wine,

Which while you taste so native seems,
So bounteous, so free,
You cannot comprehend its worth
Nor its infrequency.

· 436 ·

"SHALL I take thee?" the poet said
To the propounded word.
"Be stationed with the candidates
Till I have further tried."

The poet probed philology
And when about to ring
For the suspended candidate,
There came unsummoned in

That portion of the vision
The word applied to fill.
Not unto nomination
The cherubim reveal.

· 437 ·

IF EVER the lid gets off my head
And lets the brain away
The fellow will go where he belonged
Without a hint from me;

And the world, if the world be looking on,
Will see how far from home
It is possible for sense to live,
The soul there all the time.

· 438 ·

THE spirit is the conscious ear,
We actually hear
When we inspect that's audible
That is admitted here.

For other purposes, as sound,
There hangs a minor ear
Outside the castle that contain,
The other only hear.

· 439 ·

WHO goes to dine must take his feast
Or find the banquet mean;
The table is not laid without
Till it is laid within.

For pattern is the mind bestowed
That, imitating her,
Our most ignoble services
Exhibit worthier.

· 440 ·

To SEE the summer sky
Is poetry
Though never in a book it lie.
True poems flee.

· 441 ·

THE spry arms of the wind
If I could crawl between,
I have an errand imminent
To an adjoining zone.

I should not care to stop,
My process is not long—
The wind could wait without the gate
Or stroll the town among—

To ascertain the house,
And if the soul's within,
And hold the wick of mine to it
To light, and then return.

· 442 ·

THIS is a blossom of the brain,
A small italic seed
Lodged by design or happening—
The spirit fructified.

Shy as the wind of his chambers,
Swift as a freshet's tongue,
So of the flower of the soul,
Its process is unknown.

When it is found, a few rejoice,
The wise convey it home,
Carefully cherishing the spot
If other flower become.

When it is lost, that day shall be
The funeral of God,
Upon His breast a closing soul,
The flower of our Lord.

· 443 ·

IDEALS are the fairy oil
With which we help the wheel,
But when the vital axle turns
The eye rejects the oil.

· 444 ·

BECAUSE my brook is fluent
I know 'tis dry;
Because my brook is silent
It is the sea,

And startled at its rising
I try to flee
To where the strong assure me
Is "no more sea."

· 445 ·

The well upon the brook
Were foolish to depend;
Let brooks renew of brooks,
But wells of failless ground!

· 446 ·

Estranged from beauty none can be
For beauty is infinity,
And power to be finite ceased
When fate incorporated us.

· 447 ·

The truth is stirless. Other force
May be presumed to move.
This then is best for confidence—
When oldest cedars swerve

And oaks unclinch their fists,
And mountains feeble lean,
How excellent a body
That stands without a bone!

How vigorous a force
That holds without a prop!
Truth stays herself, and every man
That trusts her, boldly up.

· 448 ·

A MAN may drop a remark,
In itself a quiet thing,
That may furnish the fuse unto a spark
In dormant nature lain.

Let us deport with skill,
Let us discourse with care,
Powder exists in charcoal
Before it exists in fire.

· 449 ·

TELL all the truth but tell it slant,
Success in circuit lies,
Too bright for our infirm delight
The truth's superb surprise;

As lightning to the children eased
With explanation kind,
The truth must dazzle gradually
Or every man be blind.

· 450 ·

LIFT it, with the feathers
Not alone we fly!
Launch it, the aquatic
Not the only sea!

Advocate the azure
To the lower eyes;
He has obligation
Who has paradise.

· 451 ·

ONCE more my now bewildered dove
Bestirs her puzzled wings;
Once more her mistress on the deep
Her troubled question flings;

Thrice to the floating casement
The Patriarch's bird returned—
Courage, my brave Columba,
There may yet be land!

· 452 ·

THE fascinating chill that music leaves
Is earth's corroboration
Of ecstasy's impediment;
'Tis rapture's germination

In timid and tumultuous soil,
A fine estranging creature
To something upper wooing us,
But not to our Creator.

· 453 ·

DYING at my music!
Bubble! Bubble!
Hold me till the octave's run!
Quick! Burst the windows!
Ritardando!
Phials left, and the sun!

· 454 ·

Better than music, for I who heard it,
I was used to the birds before;
This was different, 'twas translation
Of all tunes I knew, and more;

'Twasn't contained like other stanza,
No one could play it the second time
But the composer, perfect Mozart,
Perish with him that keyless rhyme!

So children, assured that brooks in Eden
Bubbled a better melody,
Quaintly infer Eve's great surrender,
Urging the feet that would not fly.

Children matured are wiser, mostly,
Eden a legend dimly told,
Eve and the anguish grandame's story—
But I was telling a tune I heard.

Not such a strain the church baptizes
When the last saint goes up the aisles,
Not such a stanza shakes the silence
When the redemption strikes her bells.

Let me not lose its smallest cadence,
Humming for promise when alone,
Humming until my faint rehearsal
Drop into tune around the throne!

· 455 ·

The beggar at the door for fame
Were easily supplied,
But bread is that diviner thing,
Disclosed to be denied.

· 456 ·

A CLOVER's simple fame
Remembered of the cow
Is sweeter than enameled realms
Of notoriety.

Renown perceives itself
And that profanes the flower;
The daisy that has looked behind
Has compromised its power.

· 457 ·

FAME is the one that does not stay,
Its occupant must die,
Or out of sight of estimate
Ascend incessantly,

Or be that most insolvent thing,
A lightning in the germ;
Electrical the embryo
Or findless is the flame.

· 458 ·

JUST as he spoke it from his hands
This edifice remain;
A turret more, a turret less,
Dishonor his design.

According as his skill prefer
It perish or endure,
Content, soe'er it ornament
His absent character.

· 459 ·

FAME is the tint that scholars leave
Upon their setting names—
The iris not of occident
That disappears as comes.

· 460 ·

HE WHO in himself believes
Fraud cannot presume.
Faith is constancy's result
And assumes, from home,

Cannot perish, though it fail
Every second time,
But defaced vicariously
For some other shame.

· 461 ·

FAME of myself to justify!
All other plaudit be
Superfluous, an incense
Beyond necessity.

Fame of myself to lack, although
My name be else supreme,
This were an honor honorless,
A futile diadem.

· 462 ·

THE first we knew of him was death,
  The second was renown;
Except the first had justified
  The second had not been.

· 463 ·

ALL men for honor hardest work
But are not known to earn,
Paid after they have ceased to work,
In infamy or urn.

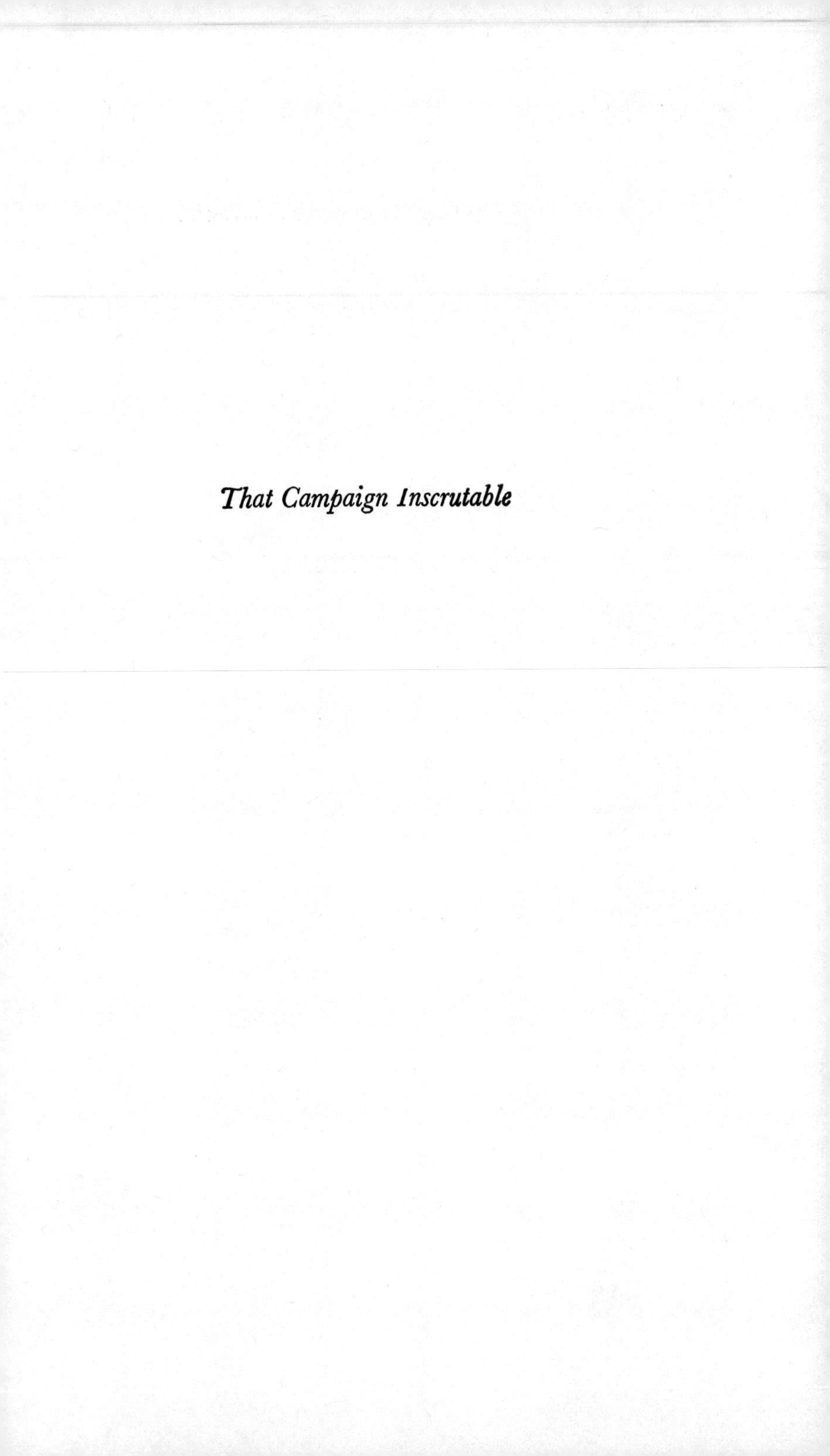

That Campaign Inscrutable

· 464 ·

'TWAS fighting for his life he was,
That sort accomplish well,
The ordnance of vitality
Is frugal of its ball;

It aims once, kills once, conquers once—
There is no second war
In that campaign inscrutable
Of the interior.

· 465 ·

THE life we have is very great;
The life that we shall see
Surpasses it we know because
It is infinity.

But when all space has been beheld
And all dominion shown,
The smallest human heart's extent
Reduces it to none.

· 466 ·

THE sun is gay or stark
According to our deed;
If merry, he is merrier;
If eager for the dead

Or an expended day
He helped to make too bright,
His mighty pleasure suits us not,
It magnifies our freight.

· 467 ·

Somewhat to hope for,
Be it ne'er so far,
Is capital against
Despair.

Somewhat to suffer,
Be it ne'er so keen,
If terminable, may
Be borne.

· 468 ·

There is a strength in knowing that it can be borne
Although it tear.
What are the sinews of such cordage for
Except to bear?
The ship might be of satin had it not to fight.
To walk on tides requires cedar feet.

· 469 ·

Could hope inspect her basis
Her craft were done,
Has a fictitious charter
Or she is none,

Balked in the vastest instance
But to renew,
Felled by but one assassin,
Prosperity.

· 470 ·

THE way hope builds his house,
It is not with a sill,
Nor rafter has that edifice
But only pinnacle;

Abode in as supreme,
This superficies,
As if it were of ledges smit
And mortised with the laws.

· 471 ·

THE service without hope
Is tenderest, I think,
Because 'tis unsustained
By end-rewarded work;

Has impetus of gain,
And impetus of goal;
There is no diligence like that
That knows not an until.

· 472 ·

A SOLEMN thing within the soul
To feel itself get ripe
And golden hang, while farther up
The Maker's ladders stop,
And in the orchard far below
You hear a being drop;

A wonderful, to feel the sun
Still toiling at the cheek
You thought was finished; cool of eye,
And critical of work,
He shifts the stem a little
To give your core a look;

But solemnest to know
Your chance in harvest moves
A little nearer; every sun
The single, to some lives.

· 473 ·

THE soul has bandaged moments
When too appalled to stir;
She feels some ghastly fright come up
And stop to look at her,
Salute her with long fingers,
Caress her freezing hair,
Sip, goblin, from the very lips
The lover hovered o'er—
Unworthy that a thought so mean
Accost a theme so fair.

The soul has moments of escape
When, bursting all the doors,
She dances like a bomb abroad,
And swings upon the hours

As do the bee, delirious borne,
Long dungeoned from his rose,
Touch liberty—then know no more
But noon and paradise.

The soul's retaken moments
When, felon, led along
With shackles on the pluméd feet
And rivets in the song,
The horror welcomes her again—
These are not brayed of tongue.

· 474 ·

NATURE sometimes sears a sapling,
Sometimes scalps a tree;
Her green people recollect it
When they do not die.

Fainter leaves to further seasons
Dumbly testify;
We who have the souls die oftener,
Not so vitally.

· 475 ·

A PANG is more conspicuous in spring
In contrast with the things that sing—
Not birds entirely, but minds,
Minute effulgences and winds.

When what they sung for is undone
Who cares about a bluebird's tune?
Why, resurrection had to wait
Till they had moved a stone!

· 476 ·

It is easy to work when the soul is at play,
But when the soul is in pain,
The hearing him put his playthings up
Makes work difficult then.

It is simple to ache in the bone or the rind,
But gimlets among the nerve
Mangle daintier, terribler,
Like a panther in the glove.

· 477 ·

As one does sickness over
In convalescent mind,
His scrutiny of chances
By blessèd health obscured;

As one rewalks a precipice,
And whittles at the twig
That held him from perdition
Sown sidewise in the crag;

A custom of the soul
Far after suffering,
Identity to handle,
For evidence 't has been.

· 478 ·

Dreams are the subtle dower
That make us rich an hour,
Then fling us poor
Out of the purple door
Into the precinct raw
Possessed before.

· 479 ·

None who saw it ever told it,
'Tis as hid as death,
Had for that specific treasure
A departing breath.

Surfaces may be invested.
Did the diamond grow
General as the dandelion,
Would you seek it so?

· 480 ·

Of the heart that goes in
And closes the door
Shall the playfellow heart complain,
Though the ring is unwhole,
And the company broke
Can never be fitted again?

· 481 ·

The heart has narrow banks;
It measures like the sea
In mighty, unremitting bass
And blue monotony,

Till hurricane bisect,
And as itself discerns
Its insufficient area,
The heart convulsive learns

That calm is but a wall
Of unattempted gauze
An instant's push demolishes,
A questioning dissolves.

· 482 ·

HER sweet weight on my heart a night
Had scarcely deigned to lie,
When, stirring for belief's delight,
My bride had slipped away.

If 'twas a dream, made solid just
The heaven to confirm,
Or if myself were dreamed of her,
The wisdom to presume

With Him remain, Who unto me
Gave, even as to all,
A fiction superseding faith
By so much as 'twas real.

· 483 ·

TALK not to me of summer trees!
The foliage of the mind
A tabernacle is for birds
Of no corporeal kind;

And winds do go that way at noon
To their ethereal homes,
Whose bugles call the least of us
To undepicted realms.

· 484 ·

WE introduce ourselves
To planets and to flowers,
But with ourselves have etiquettes,
Embarrassments and awes.

· 485 ·

EMBARRASSMENT of one another
And God
Is revelation's caution.
Aloud
Is nothing that is chief,
But still.
Divinity dwells under seal.

· 486 ·

DEATH's waylaying not the sharpest
Of the thefts of time;
There marauds a sorer robber,
Silence is his name.

No assault nor any menace
Doth betoken him,
But from life's consummate cluster
He supplants the balm.[26]

· 487 ·

THE words the happy say
Are paltry melody;
But those the silent feel
Are beautiful.

[26] First published in *Great American Girls* by Kate Dickinson Sweetser, 1931, p. 135.

· 488 ·

THERE is no silence in the earth so silent
  As that endured
Which, uttered, would discourage nature
  And haunt the world.

· 489 ·

ABSENCE disembodies, so does death,
Hiding individuals from the earth;
Superstition helps, as well as love;
Tenderness decreases as we prove.

· 490 ·

THE loneliness one dare not sound,
And would as soon surmise
As in its grave go plumbing
To ascertain the size;

The loneliness whose worst alarm
Is lest itself should see,
And perish from before itself
For just a scrutiny;

The chasm not to be surveyed,
But skirted in the dark,
With consciousness suspended,
And being under lock—

I fear me this is loneliness.
The Maker of the soul
Its caverns and its corridors
Illuminate or seal.

· 491 ·

Shame is the shawl of pink
In which we wrap the soul
To keep it from infesting eyes,
The elemental veil

Which helpless nature drops
When pushed upon a scene
Repugnant to her probity;
Shame is the tint divine.

· 492 ·

Patience has a quiet outer;
Patience, look within,
Is an insect's futile forces,
Infinites between,

'Scaping one against the other
Fruitlesser to fling;
Patience is the smile's exertion
Through the quivering.

· 493 ·

Grief is a mouse,
And chooses wainscot in the breast
For his shy house,
And baffles quest.

Grief is a thief,
Quick startled, pricks his ear
Report to hear of that vast dark
That swept his being back.

Grief is a juggler,
Boldest at the play,
Lest if he flinch,
The eye that way

Pounce on his bruises,
One, say, or three.
Grief is a gourmand,
Span his luxury.

Best grief is tongueless—
Before he'll tell,
Burn him in the public square,
His embers will,

Possibly. If they refuse
How then know,
Since a rack couldn't coax
A syllable now.

· 494 ·

THERE comes an hour when begging stops,
When the long-interceding lips
  Perceive their prayer is vain.

"Thou shalt not" is a kinder sword
Than from a disappointing God,
  "Disciple, call again."

· 495 ·

I HAVE never seen volcanoes,
But when travelers tell
How those old phlegmatic mountains,
Usually so still,

Bear within appalling ordnance,
Fire and smoke and gun,
Taking villages for breakfast,
And appalling men,

If the stillness is volcanic
In the human face
When upon a pain Titanic
Features keep their place;

If at length the smouldering anguish
Will not overcome,
And the palpitating vineyard
In the dust be thrown;

If some loving antiquary
On Resumption morn
Will not cry with joy, "Pompeii!"
To the hills return!

· 496 ·

THE joy that has no stem nor core,
Nor seed that we can sow,
Is edible to longing,
But ablative to show.

By fundamental palates
Those products are preferred
Impregnable to transit
And patented by pod.

· 497 ·

BLISS is the plaything of the child,
The lever of the man,
The sacred stealth of boy and girl,
Indict it if we can!

· 498 ·

In many and reportless places
We feel a joy
Reportless, also, but sincere as nature
Or Deity.

It comes without a consternation,
Dissolves the same,
But leaves a sumptuous destitution
Without a name.

Profane it by pursuit we cannot,
It has no home,
Nor we who, having once waylaid it,
Thereafter roam.

· 499 ·

Purple is fashionable twice—
This season of the year
And when a soul perceives itself
To be an emperor.

· 500 ·

Delight's despair at setting
Is that delight is less
Than the sufficing longing
That so impoverish.

Enchantment's perihelion
Mistaken oft has been
For the authentic orbit
Of its anterior sun.

· 501 ·

LEST this be heaven indeed
An obstacle is given
That always gauges a degree
Between ourself and heaven.

· 502 ·

SWEET skepticism of the heart
That knows and does not know,
And tosses like a fleet of balm
Affronted by the snow,

Invites and then retards the truth
Lest certainty be sere
Compared with the delicious throe
Of transport thrilled with fear.

· 503 ·

A STAGNANT pleasure like a pool
That lets its rushes grow
Until they heedless tumble in
And make the water slow,

Impeding navigation bright
Of ripples going down—
Yet even this shall rouse itself
When freshets come along.

· 504 ·

SUCH is the strength of happiness
The least can lift a ton
Assisted by its stimulus;
Who misery sustain

No sinew can afford,
The cargo of themselves
Too infinite for consciousness'
Benumbed abilities.

· 505 ·

THERE is an arid pleasure
As different from joy
As frost is different from dew;
Like element are they,

Yet one rejoices flowers,
And one the flowers abhor;
The finest honey curdled
Is worthless to the bee.

· 506 ·

THE auctioneer of parting,
His "Going, going, gone,"
Shouts even from the crucifix
And brings his hammer down.

He only sells the wilderness.
The prices of despair
Range from a single human heart
To two—not any more.

· 507 ·

THE whole of it came not at once,
'Twas murder by degrees,
A thrust—and then for life a chance
The bliss to cauterize.

The cat reprieves the mouse
She eases from her teeth
Just long enough for hope to tease,
Then mashes it to death.

'Tis life's award to die,
Contenteder if once,
Than dying half, then rallying
For consciouser eclipse.

· 508 ·

FACTS by our side are never sudden
Until they look around,
And then they scare us like a specter
Protruding from the ground.

The height of our portentous neighbor
We never know
Till summoned to his recognition
By an adieu—

Adieu till when the wise cannot conjecture;
The bravest die
As ignorant of their resumption
As you or I.

· 509 ·

Crumbling is not an instant's act,
A fundamental pause;
Dilapidation's processes
Are organized decays.

'Tis first a cobweb on the soul,
A cuticle of dust,
A borer in the axis,
An elemental rust.

Ruin is formal, devil's work,
Consecutive and slow—
Fail in an instant no man did,
Slipping is crash's law.

· 510 ·

A doubt if it be us
Assists the staggering mind
In an extremer anguish
Until it footing find;

An unreality is lent,
A merciful mirage,
That makes the living possible
While it suspends the lives.

· 511 ·

One anguish in a crowd,
A minor thing it sounds
And yet, unto the single doe
Attempted of the hounds

'Tis terror as consummate
As legions of alarm
Did leap full-flanked upon the host;
'Tis units make the swarm.

A small leech on the vitals,
The sliver in the lung,
The bung out of an artery,
Are scarce accounted harms,

Yet mighty by relation
To that repealless thing,
A being, impotent to stop
When once it has begun!

· 512 ·

As FROST is best conceived
By force of its result,
Affliction is inferred
By subsequent effect.

If when the sun reveal,
The garden keep the gash,
If as the days resume,
The wilted countenance

Cannot efface the crease
Or counteract the stain,
Presumption is, vitality
Was somewhere put in twain.

· 513 ·

ONE crucifixion is recorded only;
How many be
Is not affirmed of mathematics
Or history.

One Calvary exhibited to stranger;
As many be
As persons or peninsulas.
Gethsemane

Is but a province in the being's center;
India,
For journey or crusade's achieving,
Too near.

Our Lord indeed bore compound witness,
And yet,
There's newer, nearer crucifixion
Than that.

· 514 ·

ONE crown not any seek,
And yet the highest head
Its isolation coveted,
Its stigma deified.

While Pontius Pilate lives,
In whatsoever hell,
That coronation pierces him.
He recollects it well.

· 515 ·

TIME does go on,
I tell it gay
To those who suffer now;
They shall survive!
There is a sun!
They don't believe it now.

· 516 ·

"FAITHFUL to the end," amended
From the heavenly clause—
Lucrative indeed the offer,
But the heart withdraws.

"I will give," the base proviso.
Spare your "Crown of Life"!
Those it fits too fair to wear it—
Try it on yourself![27]

[27] A somewhat different version of this poem was published in *The New England Quarterly*, April, 1932:

"Faithful to the end" amended
From the heavenly clause,
Constancy with a proviso
Constancy abhors.

"Crowns of life" are servile prizes
To the stately heart.
Given for the giving, solely,
No emolument.

· 517 ·

An honest tear
Is durabler than bronze.
This cenotaph
May each that dies.

Reared by itself
No deputy suffice.
Gratitude bears
When obelisk decays.

An Ablative Estate

· 518 ·

THAT it will never come again
Is what makes life so sweet.
Believing what we don't believe
Does not exhilarate.

That if it be, it be at best
An ablative estate,
This instigates an appetite
Precisely opposite.

· 519 ·

CONTAINED in this short life
Are magical extents—
The soul returning soft at night
To steal securer thence
As children strictest kept
Turn soonest to the sea
Whose nameless fathoms slink away
Beside infinity.

Contained in this short life
Are terrible extents
Discernible to not a friend
Except omnipotence—
A friend too straight to stoop,
Too distant to be seen;
"Come unto me," enacted how,
With firmaments between?

· 520 ·

How much the present moment means
To those who've nothing more—
The dog, the tramp, the atheist,
Stake an entire store

Upon a moment's shallow rim,
While their commuted feet
The torrents of eternity
Do all but inundate.

· 521 ·

In this short life
That only lasts an hour,
How much, how little,
Is within our power!

· 522 ·

Did life's penurious length
Italicize its sweetness,
The men that daily live
Would stand so deep in joy

That it would clog the cogs
Of that revolving reason
Whose esoteric belt
Protects our sanity.

· 523 ·

SUMMER is shorter than any one,
Life is shorter than summer;
Seventy years is spent as quick
As an only dollar.

Sorrow is courteous and stays,
See how well we spurn him,
Equally to abhor delight,
Equally retain him.

· 524 ·

UNCERTAIN lease develops luster
On time;
Uncertain grasp, appreciation
Of sum.

The shorter fate is oftener the chiefest
Because
Inheritors upon a tenure
Prize.

· 525 ·

How human nature dotes
On what it can't detect!
The moment that a plot is plumbed
Prospective is extinct.

Prospective is the friend
Reserved for us to know
When constancy is clarified
Of curiosity.

Of subjects that resist,
Redoubtablest is this:
Where go we? Go we anywhere?
Creation after this?

· 526 ·

UNTO the whole how add?
Has "all" a further realm,
Or utmost an ulterior?
Oh, subsidy of balm!

· 527 ·

WHEN we stand on the tops of things
And like the trees look down,
The smoke all cleared away from it
And [sunset][28] on the scene

Just laying light, no soul will wink
Except it have the flaw;
The sound ones like the hills shall stand
No lightning drives away.

The perfect nowhere be afraid,
They bear their tranquil heads
When others dare not go at noon,
Protected by their deeds.

The stars dare shine occasionally
Upon a spotted world,
And suns go surer for their proof,
As if an axle held.

[28] As no copy of this poem in Emily's handwriting is at present accessible, I have supplied the word "sunset" to fill a blank in the copy made by Mrs. Todd.

· 528 ·

BETWEEN the form of life and life
The difference is as big
As liquor at the lip between
And liquor in the jug;

The latter excellent to have,
But for ecstatic need
The corkless is superior—
I know, for I have tried.

· 529 ·

THE things that never can come back are several—
Childhood, some forms of hope, the dead;
But joys, like men, may sometimes make a journey
  And still abide.

We do not mourn for traveler or sailor,
Their routes are fair,
But think, enlarged, of all that they will tell us
  Returning here.

"Here!" There are typic heres, foretold locations,
The spirit does not stand,
Himself at whatsoever fathom
  His native land.

· 530 ·

"GO TELL it"—what a message!
To whom is specified.
Not murmur, not endearment,
But simply we obeyed—

Obeyed a lure, a longing?
Oh, Nature, none of this!
"To law," said sweet Thermopylae,
"Convey my dying kiss."

· 531 ·

YESTERDAY is history
'Tis so far away.
Yesterday is poetry,
'Tis philosophy.

Yesterday is mystery.
Where it is today
While we shrewdly speculate
Flutter both away.

· 532 ·

A PIT—but heaven over it,
And heaven beside,
And heaven abroad,
And yet—a pit,
With heaven over it.

To stir would be to slip,
To look would be to drop,
To dream, to sap the prop
That holds my chances up.
Ah, pit! With heaven over it!

The depth is all my thought,
I dare not ask my feet;
'Twould start us where we sit
So straight you'd scarce suspect
It was a pit, with fathoms under it,

It's circuit just the same:
Seed, summer, tomb.
Who's doom—
To whom?

· 533 ·

WE LOSE because we win.
Gamblers,
Recollecting which,
Toss their dice again!

· 534 ·

IF WRECKED upon the shoal of thought
How is it with the sea?
The only vessel that is shunned
Is safe simplicity.

· 535 ·

THAT sacred closet when you sweep
Entitled "Memory,"
Select a reverential broom
And do it silently.

'Twill be a labor of surprise,
Besides identity
Of other interlocutors
A probability.

August the dust of that domain,
Unchallenged let it lie;
You cannot supersede itself,
But it can silence you.

· 536 ·

THROUGH those old grounds of memory
The sauntering alone
Is a divine intemperance
A prudent man would shun.

Of liquors that are vended
'Tis easy to beware,
But statutes do not meddle
With the internal bar.

Pernicious as the sunset,
Permitting to pursue
But impotent to gather,
The tranquil perfidy

Alloys our firmer moments
With that severest gold,
Convenient to the longing
But otherwise withheld.

· 537 ·

NO PASSENGER was known to flee
Who lodged a night in memory;
That wily subterranean inn
Contrives that none go out again.

· 538 ·

TO FLEE from memory
Had we the wings,
Many would fly,
Inured to slower things.

Birds with surprise
Would scan the mighty van
Of men escaping
From the mind of man.

· 539 ·

You cannot make remembrance grow
When it has lost its root.
The tightening the soil around
And setting it upright

Deceives perhaps the universe
But not retrieves the plant;
Real memory, like cedar feet,
Is shod with adamant.

Nor can you cut remembrance down
When it shall once have grown,
Its iron buds will sprout anew
However overthrown.

· 540 ·

Civilization spurns the leopard!
Was the leopard bold?
Deserts never rebuked her satin,
Ethiop her gold.

Tawny her customs she was conscious,
Spotted, her dun gown,
This was the leopard's nature, Signor,
Need a keeper frown?

Pity the pard that left her Asia!
Memories of palm
Cannot be stifled with narcotic,
Nor suppressed with balm.

· 541 ·

To UNDERTAKE is to achieve,
Be undertaking blent
With fortitude of obstacle
And toward encouragement.

That fine suspicion natures must
Permitted to revere
Departed standards and the few
Criterion sources here.[29]

· 542 ·

WHAT we see we know somewhat,
Be it but a little;
What we don't surmise, we do,
Though it shows so fickle.

I shall vote for lands with locks,
Granted I can pick 'em,
Transport's doubtful dividend,
Patented by Adam.

· 543 ·

BEST things dwell out of sight—
The pearl, the just, our thought;

Most shun the public air
Legitimate and rare;

The capsule of the wind,
The capsule of the mind,

Exhibit here as doth a burr;
Germ's germ be where?

[29] Published in *The New England Quarterly*, April, 1932.

· 544 ·

THE days that we can spare
Are those a function die,
Or friend, or nature, stranded then
In our economy.

Our estimates a scheme,
Our ultimates a sham,
We let go all of time without
Arithmetic of him.[30]

· 545 ·

BY A departing light
We see acuter quite
Than by a wick that stays.

There's something in the flight
That clarifies the sight
And brims the rays.

· 546 ·

SMILING back from coronation
May be luxury,
On the heads that started with us—
Being's peasantry—

Recognizing in procession
Ones we former knew
When ourselves were also dusty
Centuries ago,

[30] Published in *The New England Quarterly*, April, 1932.

Had the triumph no conviction
Of how many be
Stimulated by the contrast
Unto misery.

· 547 ·

REPORTLESS subjects, to the quick
Continual addressed,
But foreign as the dialect
Of Danes unto the rest.

Reportless measures, to the ear
Susceptive, stimulus,
But like an oriental tale
To others, fabulous.

· 548 ·

WHICH is the best, the moon or the crescent?
Neither, said the moon.
That is best which is not. Achieve it,
You efface the sheen.

Not of detention is fruition.
Shudder to attain.
Transport's decomposition follows—
He is prism born.

· 549 ·

WHICH is best? Heaven,
Or only heaven to come,
With that old codicil of doubt?
I cannot help esteem

The "bird within the hand"
Superior to the one
The "bush" may yield me—or may not—
Too late to choose again.

· 550 ·

IMPOSSIBILITY like wine
Exhilarates the man
Who tastes it; possibility
Is flavorless. Combine

A chance's faintest tincture,
And in the former dram
Enchantment makes ingredient
As certainly as doom.

· 551 ·

NOT to discover weakness is
The mystery of strength;
Impregnability inheres
As much through consciousness

Of faith of others in itself,
As elemental nerve.
Behind the most consummate clock
What skillful pointers move!

· 552 ·

SATISFACTION is the agent
Of satiety;
Want, a quiet commissary
For infinity.

To possess is past the instant
We achieve the joy;
Immortality contented
Were anomaly.

· 553 ·

PEACE is a fiction of our faith.
The bells a winter night
Bearing the neighbor out of sound—
That never did delight.

· 554 ·

How ruthless are the gentle!
How cruel are the kind!
God broke his contract to his Lamb
To qualify the wind.

· 555 ·

THE bird must sing to earn the crumb;
What merit have the tune
No breakfast if it guaranty?
The rose, content may bloom

To gain renown of lady's drawer,
But if the lady come
But once a century, the rose
Superfluous become.

· 556 ·

A HOUSE upon the height
That wagon never reached,
No dead were ever carried down,
No peddler's cart approached;

Whose chimney never smoked,
Whose windows, night and morn,
Caught sunrise first and sunset last,
Then held an empty pane;

Whose fate conjecture knew,
No other neighbor did,
And what it was we never lisped
Because he never told.

· 557 ·

WHEN bells stop ringing church begins—
The positive of bells.
When cogs stop, that's circumference—
The ultimate of wheels.

· 558 ·

IN RAGS mysterious as these
The shining courtiers go,
Veiling the purple and the plumes,
Veiling the ermine so;

Smiling as they request an alms
At some imposing door,
Smiling when we walk barefoot
Upon their golden floor!

· 559 ·

"SECRETS" is a daily word
Yet does not exist;
Muffled, it remits surmise,
Murmured, it has ceased.

Dungeoned in the human breast
Doubtless secrets lie,
But that grate inviolate
Comes nor goes away

Nothing with an ear or tongue;
Secrets stapled there
Will decamp but once, and armed,
To the sepulchre.

· 560 ·

OUR little secrets slink away
Beside God's "will not tell";
He kept his word a trillion years
And might we not as well

But for the niggardly delight
To make each other stare—
Is there no sweet beneath the sun
With this that may compare?

· 561 ·

BANISH air from air,
Divide light if you dare,
  They'll meet,
While cubes in a drop
Or pellets of shape
  Fit.

Films cannot annul,
Odors return whole,
  Force flame,
And with a blonde push
Over your impotence
  Flits steam.

· 562 ·

Air has no residence, no neighbor,
No ear, no door,
No apprehension of another—
Oh, happy air!

Ethereal guest at e'en an outcast's pillow,
Essential host in life's faint wailing inn,
Later than light thy consciousness accost me
Till it depart, convoying mine.

· 563 ·

No man saw awe, nor to his house
Admitted he a man,
Though by his awful residence
Has human nature been,

Not deeming of his dread abode
Till laboring to flee,
A grasp on comprehension laid
Detained vitality.

Returning is a different route
The spirit could not show,
For breathing is the only work
To be enacted now.

"Am not consumed," old Moses wrote,
"Yet saw Him face to face."
That very physiognomy
I am convinced was this.

· 564 ·

POWER is a familiar growth,
Not foreign, not to be,
Beside us like a bland abyss
In every company;

Escape it, there is but a chance
When consciousness and clay
Lean forward for a final glance—
Disprove that and you may.

· 565 ·

How many schemes may die
In one short afternoon
Entirely unknown
To those they most concern:

The man that was not robbed
Because by accident
He varied by a ribbon's width
From his accustomed route;

The love that would not try
Because beside the door
Some unsuspecting horse was tied
Surveying his despair.

· 566 ·

Luck is not chance, 'tis toil;
Fortune's expensive smile
  Is earned.

The father of the mine
Is that old-fashioned coin
  We spurned.

· 567 ·

Behold this little bane,
The boon of all alive,
As common as it is unknown,
The name of it is love.

To lack of it is woe,
To own of it is wound—
Not elsewhere, if in paradise,
Its tantamount be found.

· 568 ·

When a lover is a beggar
Abject is his knee;
When a lover is an owner
Different is he.

What he begged is then the beggar,
Oh, disparity!
Bread of heaven resents bestowal
Like an obloquy.

· 569 ·

How fleet, how indiscreet an one,
How always wrong is love—
The joyful little deity
We are not scourged to serve!

· 570 ·

Love is that later thing than death,
More previous than life,
Confirms it at its entrance and
Usurps it of itself;

Tastes death, the first to prove the sting,
The second, to its friend,
Disarms the little interval,
Deposits him with God.

Then hovers, an inferior guard,
Lest this belovéd charge
Need, once in an eternity,
A lesser than the large.

· 571 ·

Love can do all but raise the dead;
I doubt if even that
From such a giant were withheld
Were flesh equivalent.

But love is tired and must sleep,
And hungry and must graze,
And so abets the shining fleet
Till it is out of gaze.

· 572 ·

Floss won't save you from an abyss,
But a rope will,
Notwithstanding a rope for a souvenir
Does not look as well.

But I tell you every step is a sluice,
And every stop a well.
Now will you have the rope or the floss?
Prices reasonable.

· 573 ·

Experiment escorts us last,
His pungent company
Will not allow an axiom
An opportunity.

· 574 ·

Risk is the hair that holds the tun
Seductive in the air;
That tun is hollow, but the tun
With hundred-weights to spare,

Too ponderous to suspect the snare,
Espies that fickle chair
And seats itself to be let go
By that perfidious hair.

The "foolish tun," the critics say,
While that delusive hair,
Persuasive as perdition,
Decoys its passenger.

· 575 ·

SURPRISE is like a thrilling pungent
Upon a tasteless meat—
Alone too acrid, but combined,
An edible delight.

· 576 ·

THE riddle we can guess
We speedily despise.
Not anything is stale so long
As yesterday's surprise.

· 577 ·

CIRCUMFERENCE, thou bride of awe,
Possessing, thou shalt be
Possessed by every hallowed knight
That dares to covet thee.

· 578 ·

TO MEND each tattered faith
There is a needle fair;
Though no appearance indicate,
'Tis threaded in the air;

And though it do not wear
As if it never tore,
'Tis very comfortable indeed,
And specious as before.

· 579 ·

UNTIL the desert knows
That water grows
His sands suffice;
But let him once suspect
That Caspian fact,
Sahara dies.

Utmost is relative,
Have not or have
Adjacent sums;
Enough, the first abode
On the familiar road
Galloped in dreams.

· 580 ·

TO ONE denied to drink
To tell what water is
Would be acuter, would it not,
Than letting him surmise?

To lead him to the well
And let him hear it drip,
Remind him would it not somewhat
Of his condemnéd lip?

· 581 ·

WONDER is not precisely knowing,
And not precisely knowing not,
A beautiful but bleak condition
He has not lived who has not felt.

Suspense is his maturer sister;
Whether adult delight is pain
Or of itself a new misgiving—
This is the gnat that mangles men.

· 582 ·

I KNOW suspense, it steps so terse
And turns so weak away;
Besides, suspense is neighborly
When I am riding by,

Is always at the window
Though lately I descry,
And mention to my horses,
The need is not of me.

· 583 ·

As OLD as woe—how old is that?
Some eighteen thousand years.
As old as bliss—how old is that?
They are of equal years.

Together chiefly they are found,
But seldom side by side,
From neither of them though he try
Can human nature hide.

· 584 ·

GOD is indeed a jealous God,
He cannot bear to see
That we had rather not with Him
But with each other play.

· 585 ·

Too happy time dissolves itself
And leaves no remnant by;
'Tis anguish not a feather hath,
Or too much weight to fly.

· 586 ·

KILL your balm, and its odors bless you;
Bare your jessamine to the storm,
And she will fling her maddest perfume
Haply your summer night to charm.

Stab the bird that built in your bosom,
Oh, could you catch her last refrain—
Bubble—"Forgive"—"Some better"—bubble—
"Carol for him when I am gone!"

· 587 ·

How news must feel when traveling—
If news have any heart—
Alighting at the dwelling
'Twill enter like a dart!

What news must think when pondering—
If news have any thought—
Concerning the stupendousness
Of its perceiveless freight!

What news will do when every man
Shall comprehend as one,
And not in all the universe
A thing to tell remain?

· 588 ·

WITCHCRAFT was hung in history;
But history and I
Find all the witchcraft that we need
Around us every day.

· 589 ·

FAITH slips and laughs and rallies,
Blushes, if any see,
Plucks at a twig of evidence,
And asks a vane the way.

Much gesture from the pulpit,
Strong hallelujahs roll—
Narcotics cannot still the tooth
That nibbles at the soul.[31]

· 590 ·

As SUBTLE as tomorrow
That never came—
A warrant, a conviction,
Yet but a name.

[31] In Mrs. Todd's copy, this is the conclusion of an eight-stanza poem, the third of three poems combined as one: the first, "After great pain a formal feeling comes," *Further Poems of Emily Dickinson*, 1929, p. 175; the second, "This world is not conclusion," *Poems*, Third Series, 1896, p. 139. When all of Emily's manuscripts are available it may be possible to determine whether or not these three poems, now published separately, belong together.

· 591 ·

I'd rather recollect a setting
Than own a rising sun—
Though one is beautiful forgetting
And real the other one—

Because in going is a drama
Staying cannot confer;
To die divinely once a twilight
Than live is easier.

· 592 ·

None can experience stint
Who bounty have not known;
The fact of famine could not be
Except for fact of corn.

Want is a meager art
Acquired by reverse;
The poverty that was not wealth
Cannot be indigence.

· 593 ·

On that specific pillow
Our projects flit away,
The night's tremendous morrow,
And whether sleep will stay

Or usher us, a stranger,
To comprehension new,
The effort to comprise it
Is all the soul can do.

· 594 ·

You cannot take itself
From any human soul;
That indestructible estate
Enable him to dwell

Impregnable as light
That every man behold,
But take away as difficult
As undiscovered gold.

· 595 ·

To own the art within the soul,
The soul to entertain
With silence as a company
And festival maintain

In an unfurnished circumstance,
Possession is to one
As an estate perpetual,
Or a reduceless mine.

· 596 ·

Of consciousness, her awful mate,
The soul cannot be rid;
As easy the secreting her
Behind the eyes of God.

The deepest hid is sighted first,
And scant to Him the crowd;
What triple lenses burn upon
The escapade from God!

· 597 ·

As FROM the earth the light balloon
Asks nothing but release—
Ascension that for which it was,
Its soaring residence—

The spirit turns upon the dust
That fastened it so long
With indignation, as a bird
Defrauded of its song.

· 598 ·

I NEVER hear that one is dead,
Without the chance of life
Afresh annihilating me,
That mightiest belief,

Too mighty for the daily mind
That, tilling its abyss,
Had madness, had it once or twice,
The yawning consciousness.

Beliefs are bandaged, like the tongue
When terror, were it told
In any tone commensurate,
Would strike us instant dead.

I do not know the man so bold
He dare in secret place
That awful stranger, consciousness,
Look squarely in the face.

· 599 ·

THOSE, dying then, knew where they went,
They went to God's right hand;
That hand is amputated now
And God cannot be found.

The abdication of belief
Makes the behavior small –
Better an *ignis fatuus*
Than no illume at all.

PART TWO

PART TWO

Just as he spoke it from his hands
This edifice remain;
A turret more, a turret less,
Dishonor his design.

According as his skill prefer
It perish or endure,
Content soe'er it ornament
His absent character.

For one reason or another the poems in Part Two do not belong in the body of the book. Some, addressed to special persons, contain a name, or a blank where a name should be. Others are occasional bits of verse sent with gifts, usually flowers. But most of them are either incomplete—words missing, even lines—or unfinished rough drafts. Some would be placed with the finished poems except for an anticlimax at the end. Among those classified as "unfinished" a few are merely obscure.

There is also a section of short fragments, of which some may be alternative stanzas of longer poems, or lines inadvertently separated from their context long ago. Some are notes not yet incorporated in finished poems although the idea in different words may have been used. And there are fragments of yet another sort. Although these cannot be classified as poems in the usual sense, consisting of but a line or two, they are none the less complete. Length is not of the essence of finish. By Chinese standards a couplet such as this might be considered one of the most perfect poems in the book:

Soft as the massacre of suns
By evening's sabres slain.

All the fragments except "With thee in the desert," taken from my mother's copy, were found among the "scraps." Few poems in Part Two had been copied by her. She classified as "C" those she did copy and published none of them.

The poems in Part Two are arranged in three groups: Poems Incomplete or Unfinished; Fragments; and Poems Personal and Occasional. Within the third group are some bits of verse sent with gifts which might well be called, in Emily's words, "Chivalries as Tiny."

Poems Incomplete or Unfinished

· 600 ·

The sun in reining to the west
Makes not as much of sound
As cart of man in road below
Adroitly turning round.

That whiffletree of amethyst
. . . .

· 601 ·

The fairest home I ever knew
Was founded in an hour
By parties also that I knew,
A spider and a flower.

A manse of mechlin and of floss
. . . .

· 602 ·

It bloomed and dropped a single noon,
The flower distinct and red.
I, passing, thought another noon,
Another in its stead,

Will equal glow, and thought no more,
But came another day
To find the species disappeared.
The same locality,

The sun in place, no other brand
. . . .

· 603 ·

How soft a caterpillar steps!
I find one on my hand;
From such a velvet world it came,
Such plushes at command,
[Its journey never wakes my hand
Till poising for a turn][1]
Its soundless travels just arrest
My slow terrestrial eye—
Intent upon its circuit quaint
What use has it for me?

· 604 ·

THE merchant of the picturesque
A counter has and sales,
But is within or negative
Precisely as the calls.

To children he is small in price
And large in courtesy;
It suits him better than a check,
Their artless currency.

Of counterfeits he is so shy
Do one advance so near
As to behold his ample flight
. . . .

· 605 ·

THE first day that I was a life
I recollect it—how still!
The last day that I was a life
I recollect it as well.

[1] In Emily's manuscript lines 5 and 6 are crossed out.

'Twas stiller, though the first
Was still.
'Twas empty, but the first
Was full.

This was my finalest occasion,
But then,
My tenderer experiment
Toward men.

"Which choose?"
That I cannot say.
"Which choose they?"
Question memory!

· 606 ·

ARROWS enamored of his breast
Forgot to rankle there,
And venoms he mistook for balms
Renounced their character.

He bowed to nothing but delight,
Which . . .
Of injury too innocent
To know it when it passed.

· 607 ·

EACH scar I'll keep for him.
Instead I'll say of gem
In his long absence worn
A costlier one.

But every tear I bore,
Were he to count them o'er,
His own would fall so more
I'll mis-sum them.

· 608 ·

He strained my faith—did he find it supple?
Shook my strong trust—did it then yield?
Hurled my belief—but did he shatter it?
Racked with suspense, not a nerve failed!

Wrung me with anguish—must be I deserved it,
Though for what wrong he did never say,
Stabbed—while I sued his sweet forgiveness.
Jesus, it's your little "John"! Why me slay?[2]

· 609 ·

'Tis seasons since the dimpled war
In which we each were conqueror
 And each of us were slain,

And centuries 'twill be and more
Another massacre before
 So modest and so vain.

Without a formula we fought,
Each was to each the pink redoubt
. . . .

[2] In Mrs. Todd's copy the last two words are inverted.

· 610 ·

KNOWS how to forget!
But could she teach it?
'Tis the art most of all
I should like to know.

Long at its Greek
I who pored patient
Rise still the dunce
God used to know.

Mold my slow mind
To this comprehension
Oddest of sciences
Book ever con.

How to forget!
Ah, to attain it
I would give you
All other love.[3]

· 611 ·

SHE could not live upon the past
The present did not know her,
And so she sought this sweet at last
And nature gently owned her—

The mother that has not a knell
For either duke or robin,
. . . .

[3] For a different poem with the same first line see p. 116.

· 612 ·

WERE it but me that gained the height,
Were it but they that failed!
How many things the dying play,
Might they but live, they would!

· 613 ·

PERHAPS I asked too large,
I take no less than skies,
For earths grow thick as berries
In my native town.

My basket holds just firmaments,
Those dangle easy on my arm,
But smaller bundles cram.

· 614 ·

IT DON'T sound so terrible, quite, as it did.
I run it over, "Dead"—brain—"dead!"
Put it in Latin left of my school,
Seems it don't shriek so, under rule.

Turn it a little—full in the face
A trouble looks bitterest—shift it just—
Say, "When tomorrow comes this way
I shall have waded down one day."

I suppose it will interrupt me some
Till I get accustomed; but then, the tomb
Like other new things shows largest then,
And smaller by habit. It's shrewder then
Put the thought in advance a year,
How like "a fit" then murder wear![4]

[4] "On the death of Lincoln?" M.L.T.

· 615 ·

ABOVE oblivion's tide there is a pier,
And an effaceless "few" are lifted there,
Nay, lift themselves, fame has no arms
And but one smile, inlaid with balms.

[Above oblivion's tide there is a pier,
And the effaceless "few"] are scattered there;
Scattered, I say! To place them side by side,
Enough will not be found when all have died.[5]

· 616 ·

PARADISE is that old mansion
Many owned before,
Occupied by each an instant,
Then reversed the door.

Bliss is frugal of her leases,
Adam thought her thrift
Bankrupt once through his excesses—
. . . .

· 617 ·

YOU'RE right, "the way *is* narrow,"
And "difficult the gate,"
And "few there be"—correct again—
That "enter in thereat."

'Tis costly—so are purples!
'Tis just the price of breath!
With but the discount of the grave,
Termed by the brokers "death"!

[5] If the words in brackets are supplied in place of four long dashes in Emily's manuscript, this may be considered either a poem of two stanzas with the same opening lines, or a quatrain of which there are two versions.

And after that there's heaven,
The good man's dividend,
And bad men go to jail, I guess,
. . . .

· 618 ·

WHEN what they sung for is undone
Who cares about a bluebird's tune?
Why, resurrection had to wait
Till they had moved a stone.

As if the drums went on and on
To captivate the slain—
I dare not write until I hear—
When what they sung for is undone.[6]

· 619 ·

MY REWARD for being was this,
My premium, my bliss,
An admiralty less,
A scepter penniless,
And realms just dross.

When thrones accost my hands
With "Me, Miss, me,"
I'll unroll thee.
Dominions dowerless

[6] The first of these stanzas is also the second of a two-stanza poem beginning, "A pang is more conspicuous in spring," p. 245. The above fragment was written after "A pang," but both are in the writing of the eighties.

Beside this grace;
Election, vote,
The ballots of eternity
Will show just that.[7]

· 620 ·

To EARN it by disdaining it
Is fame's consummate fee.
He seeks what shuns him—look behind,
He is pursuing thee!

— — —[8]
So let us gather every day.
The aggregate of life's bouquet
Be honor and not shame.

---

[7] In another copy of this enigmatical poem the second stanza reads:

When thrones accost my hands
With "Me, Miss, me,"
I'll unroll thee—
Sufficient dynasty.
Creation powerless
To peer this grace,
Empire, state,
Too little dust
To dower so great.

The original manuscript might indicate whether this is in reality an alternative second stanza, or merely a group of alternative lines. For instance,

Dominions dowerless
Beside this grace

and

Creation powerless
To peer this grace

might be alternatives to

A scepter penniless
And realms just dross.

In any event, here is raw material on the way to becoming a great poem.

[8] Dashes appear in the manuscript.

· 621 ·

THE lassitudes of contemplation
Beget a force;
They are the spirit's still vacation
That him refresh.

The dreams consolidate in action,
What mettle fair
. . . .[9]

[9] This poem is written on a strip of paper twenty-one inches long by three-quarters of an inch wide.

Draft of a note to a friend in the margin of which is written not only the incomplete poem, "Why should we hurry? Why, indeed," poem 622, but also "Extol thee—could I—then I will," poem 322.

Though whether it's
labors lie
A Bland un-
certainty
Besets the sight —

This mighty
night —

Exists. It is — could
I — then I will
By saying nothing
then. But just the
fair — clever
ring — poisest —

Trust. Truth
those whose art
heavenly —

Fittest — brightest

Truth — smallest.

those fittest Eulogy
those thou an
heavenly , the
Perceiving
is evidence
those we an
of the sky
Partaking the
a quality
of guaranty
immortality

. 622 .

WHY should we hurry? Why, indeed,
When every way we fly
We are molested equally
By immortality?
No respite from the inference
That this which is, began,
Though where its labors lie,
A bland uncertainty
Besets the sight
This mighty night.

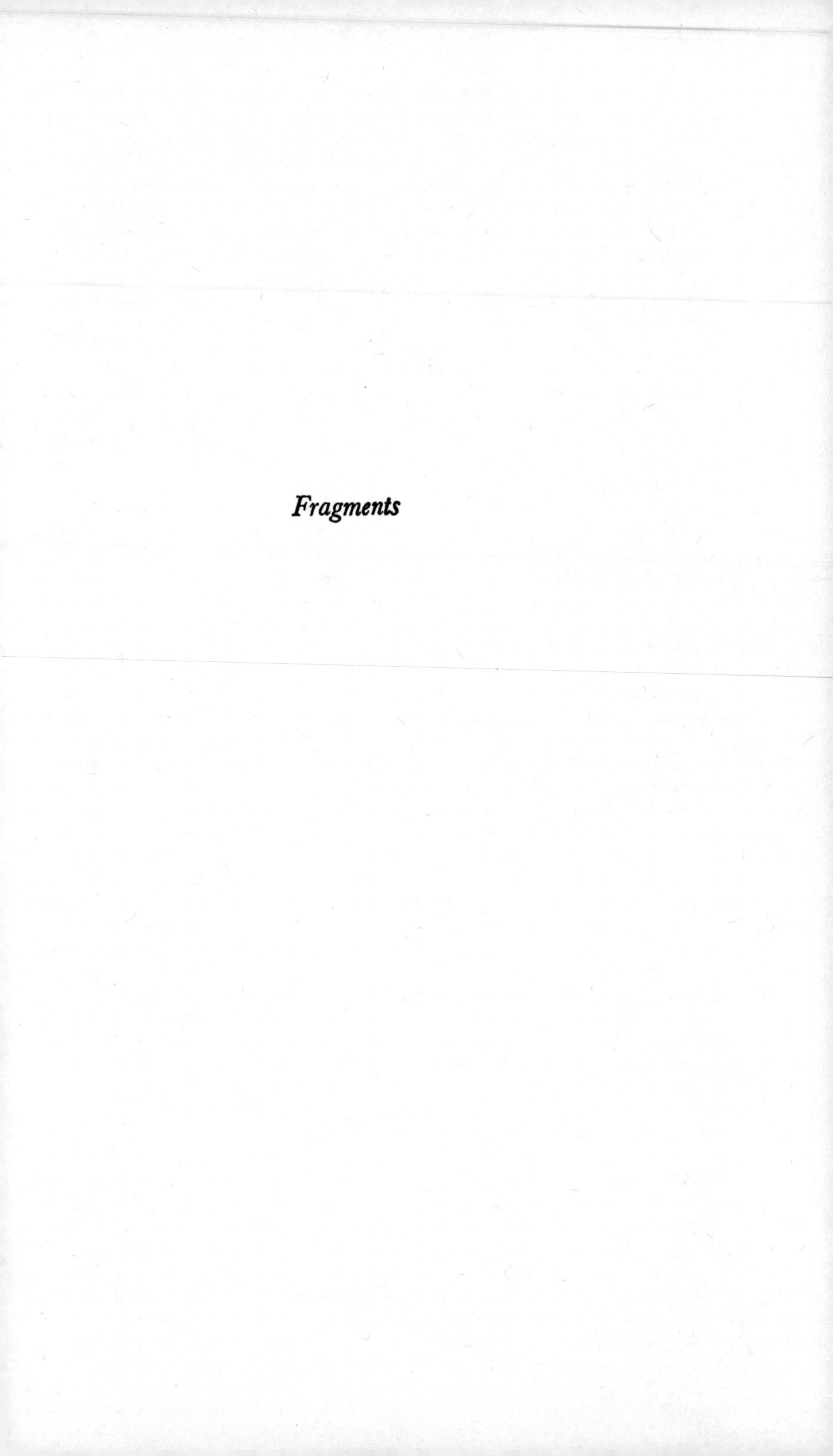

Fragments

· 623 ·

SOFT as the massacre of suns
By evening's sabres slain.

· 624 ·

SOUL, take thy risks!
With death to be
Were better than
Be not with thee![10]

· 625 ·

WITH thee in the desert!
With thee in the thirst!
With thee in the tamarind wood!
Leopard breathes—at last!

· 626 ·

LET me not thirst with this hock at my lip,
Nor beg, with domains in my pocket—

10 This fragment is written on a scrap of paper measuring less than two by four inches. On the reverse is a touching little pencil sketch of a tombstone among tall grasses.

· 628 ·

PAUSING against our palsied faces
Time's decision shook.[11]

· 629 ·

PARADISE is of the option.
Whosoever will
Dwell in Eden, notwithstanding
Adam and repeal.

· 630 ·

Is IMMORTALITY a bane
That men are so oppressed?

· 631 ·

BUT silence is infinity,
Himself have not a face.

· 632 ·

LEST they should come is all my fear
When sweet incarcerated here—

[11] This fragment, written on a slip of paper less than an inch wide, might be the germ out of which grew poem 267, "We talked with each other about each other." Both are in the handwriting of the eighties.

· 633 ·

THE blood is more showy than the breath
But cannot dance as well.

· 634 ·

SOCIETY for me my misery
Since gift of thee.

· 635 ·

OR FAME erect her siteless citadel.[12]

· 636 ·

FAME'S boys and girls who never die,
And are too seldom born—

[12] The two unrelated fragments 634 and 635 are written on the torn-off flap of an envelope.

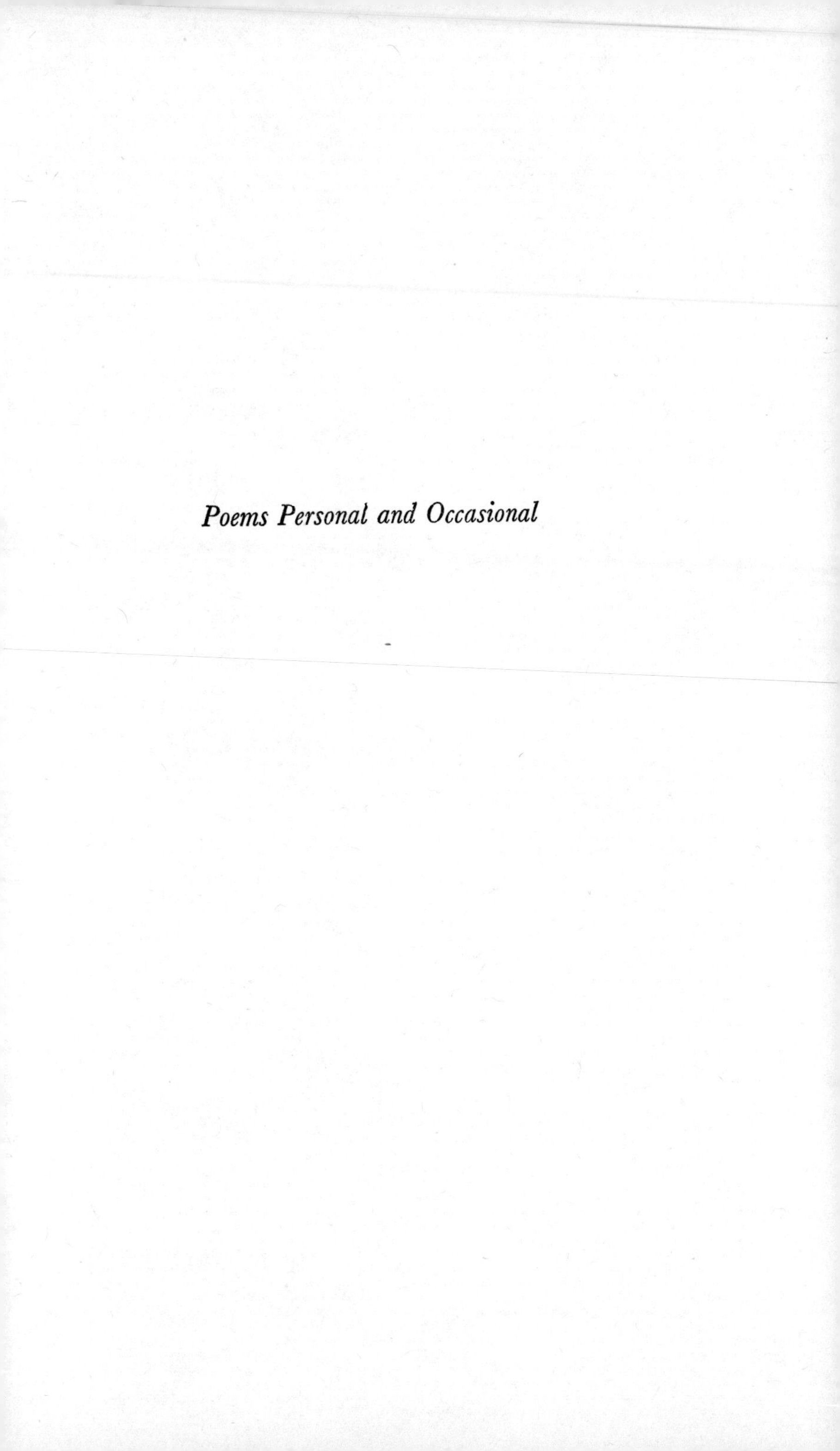

Poems Personal and Occasional

· 637 ·

YOU love me? You are sure?
I shall not fear mistake?
I shall not cheated wake
Some grinning morn
To find the sunrise left
And orchards unbereft
And Dollie[13] gone?

I need not start? You're sure
That night will never be
When, frightened, home to thee I run
To find the windows dark
And no more Dollie—mark!—
  Quite none?

Be sure you're sure you know!
I'll bear it better now
If you'll just tell me so
Than when, a little dull balm grown
Over this pain of mine,
  You sting again!

· 638 ·

DISTRUSTFUL of the gentian,
And just to turn away,
The fluttering of her fringes
Chid my perfidy.
Weary for my ———
I will singing go;
I shall not feel the sleet then,
I shall not fear the snow.

[13] "Dollie" was Emily's pet name for a friend as yet unidentified.

Flees so the phantom meadow
Before the breathless bee,
So bubble brooks in deserts
On ears that dying lie,
Burn so the evening spires
To eyes that closing go,
Hangs so distant heaven
To a hand below.[14]

· 639 ·

WHAT shall I do it whimpers so—
This little hound within the heart—
All day and night with bark and start,
And yet it will not go?

Would you untie it were you me?
Would it stop whining if to thee
I sent it, even now?

It should not tease you, by your chair,
Or on the mat, or if it dare
To climb your dizzy knee,

Or sometimes at your side to run
When you were willing—shall it come?
Tell Carlo—he'll tell me!

· 640 ·

IF THIS is "fading,"
Oh, let me immediately fade!
If this is "dying,"
Bury me in such a shroud of red!

[14] A long dash in the fifth line of the manuscript apparently indicates space for a name. This poem was written in the sixties, like "All these my banners be," p. 45, and on the back of the same sheet. That poem has a couplet at the bottom of the page. After this one also there is a short stanza, "We lose because we win," which appears as a separate poem on p. 271.

If this is "sleep,"
On such a night
How proud to shut the eye!
Good evening, gentle fellow men,
Peacock presumes to die!

· 641 ·

I SHALL not murmur if at last
The ones I loved below
Permission have to understand
For what I shunned them so—

Divulging it would rest my heart
But it would ravage theirs—
Why, Katie, treason has a voice,
But mine dispels in tears.

· 642 ·

DYING, dying in the night!
Won't somebody bring the light
So I can see which way to go
Into the everlasting snow?

And Jesus, where is Jesus gone?
They said that Jesus always came;
Perhaps he doesn't know the house—
This way, Jesus! Let him pass!

Somebody run to the great gate
And see if Dollie's coming! Wait—
I hear her feet upon the stair!
Death won't hurt now Dollie's here!

· 643 ·

I OFTEN passed the village
When going home from school,
And wondered what they did there
And why it was so still.

I did not know the year then
In which my call would come—
Earlier by the dial
Than the rest have gone.

It's stiller than the sundown,
It's cooler than the dawn,
The daisies dare to come here
And birds can flutter down.

So when you are tired,
Or perplexed, or cold,
Trust the loving promise
Underneath the mold.
Cry "It's I! Take Dollie!"
And I will enfold.

· 644 ·

BY CHIVALRIES as tiny,
A blossom or a book,
The seeds of smiles are planted
Which blossom in the dark.

· 645 ·

APOLOGY for her
Be rendered by the bee;
Herself, without a parliament,
Apology for me.

· 646 ·

Be mine the doom—
Sufficient fame
To perish in her hand!

· 647 ·

Betrothed to righteousness might be
An ecstasy discreet,
But nature relishes the pinks
Which she was taught to eat.

· 648 ·

Brother of ingots—ah, Peru,
Empty the hearts that purchased you!

· 649 ·

By such and such an offering
To Mr. So and So
The web of life is woven—
So martyrs' albums show.

· 650 ·

Dominion lasts until obtained,
Possession just as long.
But these, endowing as they flit,
Eternally belong.

How everlasting are the lips
Known only to the dew!
These are the brides of permanence,
Supplanting me and you.[15]

—Sent with leaves

[15] Published in *The New England Quarterly*, April, 1932.

· 651 ·

HER little parasol to lift
And once to let it down
Her whole responsibility—
To imitate, be mine.

A summer further I must wear,
Content if nature's drawer
Present me from sepulchral crease
As blemishless as her.
—With a morning-glory

· 652 ·

I COULD bring you jewels
Had I a mind to,
But you have enough
Of those;

I could bring you odors
From San Domingo,
Colors
From Vera Cruz.

Berries of the Bahamas have I,
But this little blaze
Flickering to itself in the meadow
Suits me more than those.

Never a fellow matched this topaz
And his emerald swing,
Dower itself for Bobadilla—
Better could I bring?
—With jewelweed

· 653 ·

I KEEP my pledge,
I was not called,
Death did not notice me.
I bring my rose,
I plight again
By every sainted bee,
By daisy called from hillside,
By bobolink from lane,
Blossom and I—
Her oath and mine—
Will surely come again!

· 654 ·

IF IT had no pencil
Would it try mine—
Worn, now, and *dull,* sweet,
Writing much to thee.

If it had no word,
Would it make the daisy
Most as big as I was
When it plucked me?[16]

· 655 ·

IT WOULD not know if it were spurned,
This gallant little flower.
How therefore safe to be a flower
If one would tamper there!

To enter, it would not aspire;
But may it not despair
That it is not a cavalier,
To dare and perish there?

[16] This slip of paper, pinned together around the stub of a pencil, was signed "Emily."

· 656 ·

Least rivers
Docile to some sea—
My Caspian, thee.

· 657 ·

Lethe in my flower
Of which they who drink
In the fadeless orchards
Hear the bobolink.

Merely flake or petal
As the eye beholds.
Jupiter! My father!
I perceive the rose!

· 658 ·

Many cross the Rhine
In this cup of mine—
Sip old Frankfort air
From my brown cigar.

· 659 ·

My heart upon a little plate
Her palate to delight
A berry or a bun would be,
Might it an apricot!

· 660 ·

My season's furthest flower
I tenderer commend
Because I found her kinsmanless—
A grace without a friend.

· 661 ·

Of Brussels it was not;
Of Kidderminster? Nay,
The winds did buy it of the woods,
They sold it unto me.

It was a gentle price
The poorest could afford;
It was within the frugal purse
Of beggar or of bird.

Of small and spicy yards,
In hue a mellow dun,
Of sunshine and of sere composed,
But princip'ly of sun.

The wind unrolled it fast,
And spread it on the ground—
Upholst'rer of the pines is he,
Upholst'rer of the pond.
—With a pine needle

· 662 ·

Partake as doth the bee,
Abstemiously;
A rose is an estate
In Sicily.

· 663 ·

SHE dwelleth in the ground
Where daffodils abide,
Her Maker her metropolis,
The universe her maid.

To fetch her grace and awe
And fairness and renown,
The firmament's—to pluck her
And fetch her thee, be mine.
—With a crocus

· 664 ·

THEIR dappled importunity
Disparage or dismiss;
The obloquies of etiquette
Are obsolete to bliss.

· 665 ·

WARM in her hand these accents lie
While faithful and afar
The grace so awkward for her sake
Its fond subjection wear.
—With a book

· 666 ·

WHERE roses would not dare to go
What heart would risk the way?
And so I send my crimson scouts
To sound the enemy.

If I should cease to bring a rose
Upon a festal day,
'Twill be because beyond the rose
I have been called away.

If I should cease to take the names
My buds commemorate,
'Twill be because death's finger
Clasps my murmuring lip.[17]

[17] This poem was chosen by Mrs. Todd in the early nineties and laid aside for eventual use as the prologue of a final series of Emily's poems.

INDEX OF FIRST LINES

Index of First Lines

Set in Linotype Baskerville
Format by A. W. Rushmore
Manufactured by The Haddon Craftsmen
Published by HARPER & BROTHERS
New York and London